920 SMI
Smith, Dian G.
Great American film
 directors

DATE DUE

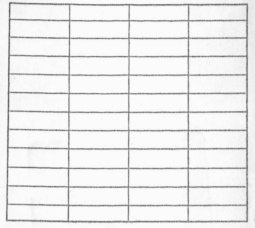

# GREAT AMERICAN FILM DIRECTORS

Also by Dian G. Smith
American Filmmakers Today
Careers in the Visual Arts:
Talking with Professionals

# GREAT AMERICAN FILM DIRECTORS

## FROM THE FLICKERS THROUGH HOLLYWOOD'S GOLDEN AGE

## DIAN G. SMITH

JULIAN MESSNER
A Division of Simon & Schuster, New York

Copyright (c) 1987 by Dian G. Smith

Published by Julian Messner,
A Division of Simon & Schuster, Inc.
Simon & Schuster Building
Rockefeller Center
1230 Avenue of the Americas
New York, New York 10020

JULIAN MESSNER and colophon are
trademarks of Simon & Schuster, Inc.

10 9 8 7 6 5 4 3 2 1
Manufactured in the United States of America

Design by Bob Silverman, Inc.

Library of Congress Cataloguing in Publication Data

Smith, Dian G.
   Great American film directors.

   Bibliography: p.
   Includes index.
   Summary: An account of the lives and accomplishments of
ten famous directors, including D.W. Griffith, John
Ford, Frank Capra, Alfred Hitchcock, and Orson Welles.
   1. Moving-picture producers and directors—United
States—Biography—Juvenile literature.  [1. Motion
picture producers and directors]  I. Title.
PN1998.A2S568   1987      791.43′0233′0922 [B] [920] 86-21838

ISBN: 0-671-50231-X

# CONTENTS

# ACKNOWLEDGMENTS

I am grateful for the vast resources of New York City for studying and viewing films: the New York Public Library, with its Library of the Performing Arts at Lincoln Center and its Donnell Film Library; the Museum of Modern Art Film Study Center; and the research library of Columbia University.

I am also grateful to my editor at Julian Messner, Jane Steltenpohl, who gave me the opportunity to write this book and helped me to improve it.

Finally, I want to thank my husband, Robert Smith, who missed many new movies during the past two years to see old ones with me; my children Ben (a Chaplin and Keaton fan), Emlen, and Rosemary (future fans); and their wise and wonderful baby-sitter, Marie-Nicole Exantus.

# INTRODUCTION

**B**etween the earliest movie mentioned in this book (D. W. Griffith's *The Adventures of Dollie)* and the most recent (John Huston's *Prizzi's Honor)* lies the entire history of American film. This short history ranges from a silent black-and-white one-reeler made less than eighty years ago to a full-sound, full-color feature-length movie made in 1985. Much of this book, however, focuses on films made between 1930 and 1950, during what has been called the Golden Age of Hollywood.

The movies were born in the late nineteenth century with the invention of the movie camera and projector. These were simply machines then, used by engineers, not artists, to record events and do tricks. D. W. Griffith was the first person to use his movie camera and his actors for the purpose of telling a story dramatically.

As the length and complexity of movies grew, so did the costs. By the 1920s, moviemaking was a business, and the studios were entertainment factories, churning out their products. They reached the height of their power during the 1930s and 1940s when audiences were hungry for entertainment, creating a huge demand for motion pictures.

It has been said that the 1940s produced some of the best and some of the worst movies ever made in America. What accounted for most of the successes was the skill of certain directors using the rich resources of the studios—the elaborate sound stages and the talented writers, actors, designers, and technicians who were on the staff or under contract. The underside of the Golden Age, which accounts for most of the terrible movies, was the control over subject matter and style that the studios demanded.

Most of the directors in this book were popular. Had they not been, the studio system would not have supported them. Yet they were able to invent new types of movies or apply a vision or style of working to the old Hollywood formulas, creating Westerns or gangster movies or screwball comedies with a personal stamp. In the eyes of the critics, however, their popularity worked against them. It was not until the 1950s, when the young "New Wave" critics in France took a close look at American movies and moviemakers, that some of these directors were taken seriously.

The selection of great American directors for this book, like any selection, could be debated. Here, for instance, Chaplin and Hitchcock are considered American while Lubitsch and von Sternberg are not. And innumerable arguments could be made about who is great or not great. Also, not every film of every director could be discussed or even mentioned. I tried to choose those that were most typical or of lasting quality.

Since its peak in 1946, the American movie industry has gone through a major crisis. Antitrust laws forced the studios during the 1950s to sell the theaters they owned. No longer did they have guaranteed outlets for their movies. At the same time the invention of television and the new suburban life-style, which kept families at home, cut into their audience. By the 1970s, independent production companies were making most movies, and the studios were only distributing them.

Another revolution is shaking the industry today, based on the new video technology. Whatever this technology bodes for the future of moviemaking, it bodes well for its past. Classic American movies used to be available only through a few museums and university film collections and were shown occasionally and unpredictably in art theaters and on late-night television. Now they can be rented inexpensively on videocassettes and shown on home TV screens. Many of the movies mentioned in this book are on videocassette already, and more become available each month. Soon a complete history of American movies and their directors will be available to everyone.

# D.W. GRIFFITH

riffith was not just a director of film master-pieces. He directed the very first film masterpieces. He changed the motion picture from a novelty sideshow, seen for five cents at a dingy nickelodeon with a tinny piano, into an art. "To watch his work," wrote film critic James Agee, "is like being witness to the beginning of melody, or the first conscious use of the lever or the wheel; the emergence, coordination, and first eloquence of language: the birth of an art."

David Wark Griffith was born on January 22, 1875, on a small dirt farm near Crestwood, Kentucky. His childhood memories are dominated by his father ("my hero"). Colonel Jake Griffith told his seven children stories about their family's noble history and about his brave deeds in the Civil War. These stories, though often far from the truth, made a deep impression on the shy,

1

sensitive David. He grew up believing he was descended from a king of Wales on one side and an immigrant English lord on the other and thinking of the Civil War as "the lost cause." *The Birth of a Nation*, his film about that period, Griffith said, "owes more to my father than it does to me."

Colonel Griffith was called Roaring Jake because of his booming voice on the battlefield. He also used that voice to read aloud from the Bible, Shakespeare, and other classics to his family and their neighbors. This was a great part of his son's education, for David attended a one-room country school where his older sister was the teacher.

Unfortunately, besides his tales, the colonel brought back from the war only some worthless Confederate bills. Never a hard worker, he now had the excuse of "war wounds" and set up post on the porch to supervise, drink, and politic.

Colonel Griffith died when David was ten, leaving his family heavily in debt. They were forced to move to a poorer farm and then to Louisville, where Mrs. Griffith ran a small boarding house. Yet memories of the beauties and hardships of Kentucky country life stayed with Griffith and appeared in many of his films.

David delivered papers after school and then, at fifteen, quit school to help support his family. He had many menial jobs, but the one he liked best was as stock boy at a bookstore where the intelligentsia of Louisville met. He would often listen in on discussions of literature and current events as he dusted the books. Customers sometimes gave him tickets to the theater and concerts, and it was at this time that he decided to become an actor and playwright. His mother, a strict Methodist, was horrified, and the only professional training he got was two years of singing lessons.

Griffith's acting career had more downs than ups. For about thirteen years, beginning when he was seventeen, he toured with countless companies that folded after varying lengths of time. The penniless Griffith would then have to make his way home, often by hopping freight cars. In between engagements, he took whatever jobs he could find, from shoveling ore out of ships to picking hops. But Griffith treasured these experiences: "It was from knowing all manner of men that I derived my most useful education." His failure as a leading man did permanent damage to his vanity, however. He considered himself ugly and tried to offset his long hook nose by always wearing wide-brimmed hats.

In 1905, he fell in love with Linda Arvidson, a young actress who had performed with him in a company in San Francisco. They got married the next year and moved to New York. He had sold a play about migratory workers and planned to support her by writing plays.

His play failed, however, and a friend suggested that he try writing for moving pictures. Like others in the legitimate theater, Griffith looked down on this new medium, but he did agree to see one. "I found it silly, tiresome, inexcusable . . . but the great interest the audience evinced impressed me."

At first he was offered only acting jobs by the movie companies. Then the Biograph Company began to buy his stories, and soon, because of the shortage of directors, he was asked to direct. His first film was *The Adventures of Dollie* (1908), about a little girl kidnapped by Gypsies and sent down a rushing stream in a barrel. He made it in two days with only one rehearsal; for his work he was paid sixty-five dollars. Yet even in this film Griffith was thinking creatively and dramatically. "I adopted 'flashback' to build suspense," he wrote. "Instead of showing a continuous view of a girl floating downstream in a barrel, I cut into the film by flashing back to incidents that contributed to the scene and explained it."

After the success of *Dollie*, Griffith was allowed to pick his own stories, actors, and locations. He also began a long collaboration with cameraman Gottlieb Wilhelm ("Billy") Bitzer. Between 1908 and 1913 he directed about 450 films for Biograph. Working fourteen hours a day, six or seven days a week, he turned out one twelve-minute and one six-minute film a week. And in the process, according to film critic Iris Barry, "Griffith discovered and laid down all the basic principles of filmmaking."

Most of Griffith's Biograph films were contemporary melodramas dealing with everyday life. He wrote some himself; others came from the story department or were borrowed from literature. Many were filled with action and had the famous "Griffith ending"—a last-minute chase. The Civil War was his favorite historical period, and he was concerned about the sufferings of the poor. In *A Corner in Wheat* (1909) a tycoon buys up the wheat crop, causing prices to soar. Griffith breaks into the scene of a grand party celebrating the tycoon's success with a tableau of poor people waiting in a bread line.

Griffith is credited with what may have been the first comedy series (the Jones comedies), the first gangster picture (*The Musketeers of Pig Alley*, 1913), the first American film spectacle (*The Massacre*, 1912, about Custer's Last Stand), and the first psychological drama (*The Avenging Conscience*, 1914).

When he left Biograph in 1913, Griffith published a newspaper advertisement claiming to have been the first to use a number of techniques: "the large or close-up figures, distant views . . . the 'switchback,' sustained suspense, the fade-out, and restraint in expression." In truth, some of these had been used before, but Griffith was the first to use them to help tell a story. He showed a close-up of a wife's face, for instance, in *After Many Years* (1908) to reveal her grief over losing her sailor husband in a shipwreck. In *The Lonedale Operator* (1911), he cut back and forth between two simultaneous events to build suspense: a telegraph operator calls desperately for help as thieves try to break into her office; meanwhile, with the cuts getting shorter and shorter, the hero races his train to her rescue, arriving just in time.

Griffith was particularly concerned with realism. With the camera so close, he urged his actors to be more "subtle and expressive" than they would be on the stage. He also experimented with realistic lighting—natural light coming through a window, for instance, and light from a fireplace. He much preferred natural settings to the studio, first using those nearby. "A beautiful sleet had covered the trees in Central Park," his wife Linda wrote, "and we hurried out to photograph it, making up the scenario on the way." Then he started taking his company on location, first to a small village in New York State and then to California.

It was after one of the California trips that his deteriorating relationship with Linda culminated in a bitter fight about his attentions to other women. They separated, but didn't divorce officially for many years. To those who knew Griffith later, it seemed strange that he had ever been married, for he was completely devoted to his work. "I believe in the motion picture not only as a means of entertainment but as a moral and educational force," he wrote.

In the course of making his first films, Griffith established a repertory company, mainly of young women, which stayed with him. He chose very young actresses, he said, because the camera is hard on the face. But he also liked the role of father figure and teacher, and the family atmosphere that was otherwise

D. W. Griffith on location with Billy Bitzer (at camera), Blanche Sweet (far left), and Dorothy Gish. *Museum of Modern Art, Film Stills Archive.*

missing from his life. Griffith was concerned about physical fitness and boxed every morning, but his favorite sport was dancing. He would often take his company for a night of dancing, and wherever they went on location, there was someone to play the piano.

Yet Griffith kept a distance from his actors and actresses and never saw a girl alone in his office. Lillian Gish, his greatest actress and oldest friend, always called him Mr. Griffith in public; he called her Miss Gish or Miss Lillian.

As a director, Griffith never used a script but would rehearse until all the actors knew their roles and the cameraman knew exactly what to do. "With his energy," said Mae Marsh, "I remember best his infinite patience. . . . He never lorded it over his players. . . . He would say, 'You understand this situation. Now let us see what you would do with it.'" He encouraged his actors to study everyone around them as models for their art. According to Lillian Gish, "We were all made to visit hospitals, insane asylums, death prisons, houses of prisoners, to catch, as he put it, humanity off guard so that we would know how to react to the various emotions we were called upon to portray."

D. W. Griffith was also a perfectionist. By 1920, when he was making *Way Down East*, he was shooting scenes thirty or forty times before he was satisfied. He supervised the editing himself and then went to the opening nights in major cities and cut further, based on audience response.

The natural extension of Griffith's editorial and photographic experiments would have been longer films, but Biograph was unwilling to finance them. The owners were horrified when *Judith of Bethulia* (1914), his first feature, an Old Testament spectacle with a large cast and elaborate sets, doubled its original budget.

In 1913 Griffith left Biograph to become head of production for Majestic-Reliance, and he took his best players with him. For this company he was expected to keep a film assembly line going ("grinding out sausages," he called it) and to train and supervise actors and directors. But he spent most of his time working on his own films, two of which were to be his great masterpieces, *The Birth of a Nation* (1915) and *Intolerance* (1916).

*The Birth of a Nation*, a story of the Civil War and Reconstruction, has been hailed as the first motion picture and one of the greatest ever made. "Mastery and tenderness of characterization, instinctive mastery of form: these were his gifts to movies," wrote critic Arlene Croce. It has also been condemned as racist because of its portrayal of blacks as either childlike or crude and lecherous, and for its glorification of the Ku Klux Klan. The motion picture was based on *The Clansman*, a violently racist contemporary novel that reinforced the attitudes with which Colonel Griffith had imbued his son. "One could not find the sufferings of our family and friends—the dreadful poverty and hardships during the war and for many years after—in the Yankee-written histories we read in school," Griffith wrote. "From all this was born a burning determination to tell some day our side of the story to the world."

To dramatize this history Griffith used a technique he had employed in *Judith* and would use in all his spectacles: focusing on a personal story. Here it is the story of two families, one northern (the Stonemans, based on Thaddeus Stevens) and one southern (the Camerons), who become entwined through friendship and love.

Griffith personally oversaw every aspect of this twelve-reel film, with its great marches, battles, and rides on horseback. He rehearsed his cast for almost two months without a written script, somehow conveying to

The Camerons (Henry B. Walthall, Mae Marsh, Spottiswoode Aiken, Josephine Crowell?, Miriam Cooper) in *The Birth of a Nation*, Epoch, 1915. *Museum of Modern Art, Film Stills Archive.*

them his fervor. For his own sense of continuity, he had the film processed every day.

In *The Birth of a Nation* Griffith was able to use to the fullest all the techniques he had developed. He used fade-ins and fade-outs as transitions. He used "masking," covering the camera lens to block off part of the image, to provide drama. A shot of a mother and her children on a hillside in the upper corner opens to reveal Sherman's troops down below, burning their farm. He told his story by moving from one narrative thread to another. This cross-cutting is especially effective in the climactic scene when the Klan races to the rescue of the Camerons. His camera was constantly on the move, whether traveling on a dolly through a farewell ball for the southern soldiers or looking down on marching troops. He also tried new techniques. He wanted close-ups of the flying hooves of the Klan's horses. Bitzer got them for him by crouching on the ground, although the side of his camera was kicked in.

Behind the technique is Griffith's innate sense of drama. In the moving scene of Ben Cameron's return to his home in the South, his mother's arm draws him in through the open doorway though she herself is unseen. Griffith also breaks the tension with touches of comedy. A love-struck hospital guard moans and sighs as Lucy Stoneman (Lillian Gish) tends the wounded soldiers.

The film was a sensation, giving new respectability to the movies. It was shown mainly in legitimate theaters, where tickets cost an unprecedented two dollars. Despite its success, Griffith was terribly upset by the charges of racism, and some critics see his next picture, *Intolerance* (1916), as a reply.

*Intolerance* is made up of four stories of injustice and prejudice and the evil caused by the self-righteous, which are intercut so that the action of one parallels or contrasts with those before and after. There are three historical sagas, each focusing on a personal story: the betrayal of Belshazzar in the sixth century B.C. by his priests and the fall of Babylon to the Persian Cyrus; the crucifixion of Christ; and the Massacre of the Huguenots on Saint Bartholomew's Day in A.D. 1572. The modern saga is filled with urban tragedies. At the end, an innocent young man (Robert Harron) is found guilty of murder and sentenced to be hanged. He is saved at the last minute when his loving wife (Mae Marsh) reaches the gallows with a pardon.

*Intolerance* had a credited cast of more than sixty, thousands of extras, and vast sets (the Babylonian set was almost half a mile long, and an army could march on its walls). Yet Griffith, with only a pocketful of notes, managed every detail himself.

In this film Griffith moved his camera more than ever before. The shot at the opening of the feast of Belshazzar, a "tracking shot," starts a quarter-mile away and moves gradually down and forward to enter the action of the city. It was taken from a 140-foot rolling tower mounted on six railroad tracks.

*Intolerance* is also admired for the emotional range of the actors, the rhythm of cutting, the composition of the shots, the dramatic use of the size and shape of the screen, and close-ups of important details. There is a brief close-up of Mae Marsh's tightly clasped hands, for instance, as she sits through her husband's trial.

Griffith invented what is now called the process shot, using an artificial sky over Babylon when the Persians attack, to provide a sense of depth and vastness. He also tinted the film more than he had ever done before—using blue for night scenes, yellow for sunny or lighted rooms, and red for the Babylonian battle at night.

But the reviews of *Intolerance* were mixed, and it was a commercial failure. Some viewers could not follow the plot. The constant movement prevented others from getting emotionally involved. And in 1916, when America was about to enter World War I, the film's pacifist theme clashed with the public spirit. This failure was a financial blow to Griffith, who had put his own money into the movie.

Before the failure of *Intolerance*, Griffith made a deal to work for Artcraft, then started on *Hearts of the World* (1915), a propaganda film the British government had asked him to make. He sent his actors to a London railroad station to observe the emotions of soldiers and civilians.

Griffith wrote the script, saying at the time that "viewed as drama, the war is disappointing." He thus chose to show the horrors of war through the stories of two American families trapped in a village in occupied France. The film was a financial success, and Griffith went on to fulfill his Artcraft commitment, though most of those films have been lost.

In 1919 Griffith made a bid for independence by beginning work on a studio of his own near Mamaroneck, New York, on Long Island Sound. He also joined with Mary Pickford, Douglas Fairbanks, and Charles Chaplin in a new distributing company called United Artists, which was to protect them from a threatened merger of producing companies. To pay for the studio and to finance his United Artist pictures he made a number of pot-boilers for First National, which got bad reviews.

*Broken Blossoms* (1919), his first picture for United Artists, was a solid hit, and it is still considered among his best. Critics of the time liked it better than *The Birth of a Nation* and *Intolerance*, praising the poetic mood Griffith created with artificial fog, special lighting effects, and tints. Griffith himself composed its musical theme. Taken from a collection of stories about the Chinese district of London, it is the tragic story of the love of a Chinese man (Richard Barthelmess) for an English girl (Lillian Gish). She is the illegitimate daughter of a violent boxer who abuses her. (He even threatens her when she can't force a smile on her sad face.) When he discovers her at the man's house, where she had been treated like a princess, he drags her home and finally beats her to death. Gish went to a mental hospital to study the hysteria she had to show in that scene.

Gish and Barthelmess also starred in Griffith's next picture, *Way Down East* (1920), which was second only to *The Birth of a Nation* in commercial success. It was a well-known theatrical melodrama written in the 1890s, which no one but Griffith thought could be revived. Anna is an innocent country girl seduced by a city playboy and deserted when she becomes pregnant. After her baby dies, she and the son of a squire for whom she is working fall in love. But when gossip about her past reaches the squire, he kicks her out into a terrible storm. She is floating down a river on a cake of ice approaching a waterfall when her lover rescues her, and all is forgiven.

Griffith used cross-cutting, as he often did, for the rescue scene. But there is also a moving scene earlier that cuts from Anna in her shabby room with her dead baby in her arms to her seducer luxuriating on his family's estate.

Griffith's career now went into decline, and his films began to be criticized as melodramatic and sentimental. A number of explanations have been given: that his artistic skill had deteriorated; that fame had made him self-conscious; that he no longer had total control of his films; that filmmaking had become too complex for him. There is also the possibility that audiences were becoming more sophisticated (film now had its first sex symbol—Theda Bara) and were no longer interested in sweet innocence.

Griffith made a weak imitation of *Broken Blossoms* (*Dream Street*, 1921) with Carol Dempster, his current flame but a limited actress. Then he made *Orphans of the Storm* (1922), a combination of an old melodrama and Dickens's *Tale of Two Cities*, which audiences liked but not well enough to pull Griffith out of his financial rut. Though some critics have praised it, film historian Lewis Jacobs called it the work of a man "no longer influencing the movies but being influenced by them." He then had two failures: another historical drama, *America* (1924), about the Revolutionary War, and *Isn't Life Wonderful* (1924), about the terrible conditions in Germany after World War I.

In desperation, Griffith was persuaded to let Lillian Gish go, as an economy measure. The result was a deep personal loneliness, for the Gishes had been a sub-

stitute family for him. Although Griffith loyally sent
money to his relatives in Kentucky, he got little love or
even attention in return. He also made a deal with
Adolph Zukor, giving up his independence on story deci-
sions, budgets, and casting to become, at the age of fifty,
just another Paramount director.

By 1927 Griffith was at the very bottom of his
career. His last three films, all with Carol Dempster, had
lost money. Paramount had released him. Now he and
Dempster separated, but he had no money to direct films
independently. He made essentially the same deal with
United Artists he had had with Paramount, and he
moved back to Hollywood. His first three films had disappointing returns, and he began drinking too much. But
the studio was willing to take a chance on his first sound
film, *Abraham Lincoln* (1930), starring Walter Huston.

By now he admitted that his drinking was an
illness, and the filming, he said, was a "nightmare of the
mind and nerves." Several trade magazines chose him as
best director of the year, but audiences did not respond
to the film and Griffith himself complained that he hadn't
had enough control and that the result was "all dry
history with no thread of romance." Again he was released.

Griffith got a small windfall in 1931 in the form of a
tax refund that allowed him to make his last film, *The
Struggle*. He made it cheaply and quickly. It is the story
of a family man who becomes a drunkard and a bum and
is finally saved and nursed to health by his loving wife
and young daughter. Although some critics now consider
it better than *Abraham Lincoln*, audiences in the midst
of the Depression were looking for light amusement, and
*The Struggle* lasted only a week in the theaters.

Griffith secluded himself in his hotel and drank.
For the next sixteen years, he lived on impossible dreams
and memories of the past. Although he was given a few

honors by the film industry and appeared occasionally in public, his work was not fully appreciated until long after his death.

His personal life was also unhappy. In 1935 he finally divorced Linda Arvidson and married Evelyn Baldwin, a twenty-four-year-old actress whose sweet appearance fit his ideal of female innocence. But the marriage was a failure, and in 1947 he moved into the Hollywood Knickerbocker Hotel, where he drank heavily in his room and roamed the streets and bars at night.

D. W. Griffith died of a cerebral hemorrhage on July 23, 1948, at the age of seventy-three, and was buried in his family's plot in Kentucky, according to his instructions. The grave remained unmarked until 1950, when the Screen Directors Guild provided a marble head-stone with a gold medallion.

# CHARLES CHAPLIN

he Little Tramp who ambles down seedy city streets in shabby, ill-fitting clothes is not merely an invented film character; he is a memory. His creator, Charles Chaplin, who has been called a genius and compared to Keats, Shelley, and Nijinsky, and who died leaving an estate worth $15 million, grew up in a London slum wearing clothes not much better than those of the famous Tramp.

Charles Spencer Chaplin was born on April 16, 1889. His father was a music-hall singer and comedian and his mother a dancer and singer. They and his mother's older son Sydney lived together fairly comfortably. But when Charlie was about two, the couple separated. His father was drinking heavily (he finally died of alcoholism in 1901), and his mother became involved with another man. When that affair ended after a couple of years, Mrs. Chaplin tried to make a living on her own. But she lost her voice and had to take up dressmaking. That failed, and when Charlie was about six, his mother began the first of several stays in hospitals and the poorhouse, while her children were sent to schools for indigent boys.

But Mrs. Chaplin had passed on to her son her theatrical skills. When Charlie was nine he worked for two years as a clog dancer and mime with a music-hall act. For two more years he did anything to make money—from selling flowers on the street to working on a printing press. Then his mother had a nervous breakdown and was put in an asylum. Somehow Charlie survived alone on the streets of London by doing odd jobs until Sydney returned from a stint at sea and took Charlie under his wing.

Though Mrs. Chaplin never fully regained her sanity, Chaplin continued to adore her. When he was a successful comedian in America, he brought her to live near him in a cottage overlooking the sea. She had stirred his interest in the theater, and "in spite of the squalor in which we were forced to live, she . . . made us feel we were not the ordinary product of poverty, but unique and distinguished."

When Sydney returned, he took his brother to various theatrical agencies, and by 1904 Charlie Chaplin was a well-known boy actor. Going to rehearsals, he wrote, "opened up a new world of technique. I had no idea there was such a thing as stagecraft—timing, pausing, a cue to turn, to sit—but it came naturally to me." He had originally wanted to be a dramatic actor but soon began to concentrate on comedy and "to enjoy hearing the bursts of laughter from the audience."

Sydney became a leading comedian with Fred Karno's troupe, England's best comic sketch company. Charlie joined this company when he was seventeen and stayed for seven years, touring Europe and America. From Karno he learned acrobatics, pantomime, and many comic gags and routines, and it was during these years that he honed his talents to perfection.

Mack Sennett, the film comedian and founder of Keystone Comedies, spotted Charlie on one of his American tours and hired him in 1914. Chaplin spent a year acting in thirty-four short films and one feature, and learning everything he could in the developing plant and the cutting room. Although his style was more natural than that of Keystone's other clowns, he was soon its most popular character, and Sennett let him direct twenty films. These had to be done in the Keystone style, however, full of slapstick and fast action and usually ending in comic violence and a chase.

Chaplin credits Sennett with teaching him how to make movies: "Although unlettered like myself, he had belief in his own taste, and such belief he instilled in me. . . . His remark that first day at the studio: 'We have no scenario—we get an idea, then follow the natural sequence of events,' had stimulated my imagination."

At Keystone, Chaplin created his famous tramp costume, although the character didn't develop fully until later. Sennett needed some gags for a film he was shooting and told Chaplin to put on comedy makeup. Chaplin chose from what was in the dressing room. In 1923, he explained the meaning of this accidental costume, which became part of the Charlie character and an important tool in his comedy: "The derby, too small, is striving for dignity. The mustache is vanity. The tightly buttoned coat and the stick and his whole manner are a gesture towards gallantry and dash and 'front.' He is trying to meet the world bravely, to put up a bluff, and he knows that, too. He knows it so well that he can laugh at himself, and pity himself a little.

When his year at Keystone was over, Chaplin was offered ten times his salary to join another company, Essanay. There he was given more freedom, a greater role in production, and three weeks instead of one to work on a film. As a result, perhaps, his fourteen Essanay films are slower paced and a little more serious. But he continued to work only from an outline. When at a loss for an idea, he would have a café set built to improvise around.

The way Chaplin usually worked with actors was to rehearse with each one separately, first showing what he wanted by playing the part himself. And he always warned them, "Don't sell it. Remember, they're peeking at you."

At Essanay, Chaplin assembled his own group of actors and technicians. The most important of these was Edna Purviance, a placid, statuesque blonde who was his leading lady for nine years in thirty-five films, and who was also his lover. Edna was a stenographer when he met her. He taught her to act, and in her he created the perfect foil for his film character. Charlie the Tramp often suffered the pangs of unrequited love, which Chaplin himself had suffered as a young man and never seemed to have forgotten.

*The Tramp* (1915) was Chaplin's first generally recognized classic and the first film in which there is a note of pathos, which would be so important to his work later. Charlie saves Edna from a gang of crooks and is rewarded by her father with a job on his farm, at which he fails miserably. (He milks the cow by pumping its tail.) When Edna's fiancé appears, the lovesick Charlie walks off alone down a long road, as he often would again.

Chaplin said he got his ideas for films by adding "the slightest twist or exaggeration" to incidents and people from everyday life. The source for *The Tramp*, he told interviewers, was a hobo he met in San Francisco and treated to lunch and a beer in exchange for conversation.

By the time his contract with Essanay was up, Charlie Chaplin was the most popular figure in American movies. Sydney signed on as his business manager and in 1916 made a lucrative deal for him with the Mutual Company. He produced twelve two-reel films in his eighteen months there, using many of the actors he had worked with in the past and adding others to his informal company.

His twelve Mutual films are better than his earlier ones. They have more highly developed plots and themes, and the humor is integrated with the story rather than thrown in. The camera work and the sets also show greater skill.

Chaplin told his cast that the set of *The Pawnshop* (1916) reminded him of "the less than good days—the seamy side of my life." This film is considered one of his best Mutuals. In it, Charlie, as an assistant in a pawnshop, creates some unforgettable scenes. In the most famous of these, a customer wants to pawn an alarm clock. Chaplin examines the clock—using a stethoscope, a dental forceps, a jeweler's loupe, a drill, and finally a can opener. Having shaken out and measured the contents, he then sweeps them into the man's hat and sadly shakes his head no.

At Mutual, Chaplin also developed the Tramp character further and heightened the pathos. The best example of this is *The Vagabond* (1916). The Tramp rescues Edna from a Gypsy family who kidnapped her as a child and who treat her like a slave. He falls in love, but loses her to a painter. While she is away with her other admirer, Charlie sets a pathetic table (an overturned metal tub), using his shirt as a tablecloth and folding the sleeves into napkins.

Critics, despite their praise, find the same faults in these films that they do in his later masterpieces—their extremely simple cinematography and negligible plots. Chaplin's instructions were always that he was to be the center of all scenes, everything else subordinated to him. "My own camera set-up is based on facilitating choreography for the actor's movements," he wrote. "The camera should not intrude." As for plots, he said, "An idea without theatrical sense is of little value. It is more important to be effective with a theatrical sense. I can be effective about nothing."

His next contract was with First National, for which he made eight films in five years. From this time on, Chaplin was to control his films completely, as author, star, producer, director, and chief editor. He took most of his actors with him and after 1918 made the films from his own studio on the outskirts of Hollywood. He aimed now, he said, to concentrate on character. The Tramp became gentler, the comedy less wild, and the other characters and settings more realistic.

Of his films from this period, four are most admired. In *A Dog's Life* (1918), he uses a parallel structure to contrast the hard street life of the Tramp with that of the mutt, Scraps. In *Shoulder Arms* (1918), he uses both realism and irony to show the life of a soldier in World War I. In one episode, Charlie, who has gotten no mail, reads a letter over the shoulder of another soldier, smiling, frowning, and sighing vicariously. His own package, when it arrives, contains a Limburger cheese so overripe he has to put on his gas mask before throwing it into the enemy trench. This film, shot during a heat wave, taught Chaplin to "loathe working outside on location because of the distraction. One's concentration and inspiration blow away with the wind."

In parts of *The Pilgrim* (1923), Chaplin is at his best. An escaped convict steals a minister's robes and is adopted mistakenly by a congregation. He delivers a sermon about David and Goliath in pantomime, taking both roles and hopping from one side of the pulpit to the other.

But one film from this period is still ranked among the greatest of all motion pictures, and that is *The Kid* (1921). It was Chaplin's first feature-length film and contains more drama and less clowning than ever before. On the screen, after the title, this description appears: "a comedy with a smile—and perhaps a tear."

*The Kid* is the story of the relationship between the Tramp and an infant he finds in the trash and takes home to raise. Some parts seem almost autobiographical, especially the Tramp's ramshackle room and the scene in which the Kid is dragged off to the orphan asylum.

Jackie Coogan, who played the Kid, was a four-year-old whom Chaplin had spotted performing with his father on the vaudeville stage. Charlie trained the boy himself, and a real bond grew between them. When Chaplin wanted Jackie to cry, he would tell him sad stories.

As always, Chaplin was a perfectionist, and although the film rambles, it has many perfectly timed scenes. In one, Jackie, having made pancakes, calls the Tramp to the table. Charlie sits up, slipping his head through a large hole in the bedspread, and arrives at the table in a makeshift dressing gown. It took two weeks and 50,000 feet of film to get that scene just right.

Chaplin traveled to Europe as a celebrity for the premiere there of *The Kid*. He had begun a campaign of self-education and was eager to meet English intellectuals and to visit, as he always did, the scenes of his childhood.

Meanwhile, Chaplin's private life was being dragged through the press, as it would be throughout his career. In 1918 he had married a pretty young actress, although they had little in common and barely knew each other. Their baby died soon after birth, and they were divorced after two years. During the 1920s, stories of Chaplin's many romances, some with famous stars, filled the newspapers. He was also called a coward because he did not enlist to fight in World War I, but at only 130 pounds, he did not meet the physical requirements for the army. He did work for the Liberty Bond campaign, however.

Even his personality came under attack. One critic accused him of being "egotistical" and "avaricious." Defenders maintained that he was merely shy and that his moodiness was related to the strain of working out his ideas. And Chaplin never denied that he had despised the poverty he lived in as a child and that he'd hated not having enough to eat or wear.

Early in 1919 Chaplin joined with D. W. Griffith, Mary Pickford, and his good friend Douglas Fairbanks to form United Artists, a company that would produce and distribute its own films. *A Woman of Paris* (1923) was his first UA film and an uncharacteristic one, in which he had only a bit part. He chose this serious story of a love triangle partly to launch Edna Purviance on a dramatic career, for she was getting too maternal-looking to play opposite the Tramp. This failed, and with typical generosity to his older players, he kept her on his payroll for the rest of her life. Meanwhile, in his attempt to "convey psychology by subtle action" he created a style that influenced other filmmakers.

Many critics consider Chaplin's next film, *The Gold Rush* (1925), his most perfect blend of comedy and pathos. And Chaplin said at the time that it was "the picture I want to be remembered by."

For the story of the Klondike Gold Rush of 1895, he used incidents from accounts of the Donner Party's tragic experiences while traveling west to California. In

Charlie Chaplin in *The Gold Rush,* United Artists, 1925. *Museum of Modern Art, Film Stills Archive.*

one scene, an allusion to their cannibalism, Charlie's starving companion sees him as a chicken and tries to catch him. In another, the roasted moccasins the Donner Party ate become Charlie's famous Thanksgiving feast of a boiled shoe. (He picks at the nails in the sole as if they were bones and eats the laces like spaghetti.) Chaplin went through about twenty pairs of licorice shoes before this scene was perfected.

Chaplin described a change in the Tramp at this time when he began to think of him as "a sort of Pierrot. With this conception I was freer to express and embellish the comedy with touches of sentiment." The gentle clown with the sad, white-painted face and baggy pantaloons of nineteenth-century French pantomime might have played Charlie's part in a scene in *The Gold Rush* in which he prepares a New Year's Eve dinner for the showgirl Georgia and her friends. While waiting, he daydreams about entertaining them with a dance of rolls, his forks kicking, turning, and spinning them about. The girls, however, carelessly forget to show up.

During the filming of *The Gold Rush*, Chaplin entered into his second disastrous marriage, again to a very young and completely incompatible actress. Three years and two sons later, during a bitter divorce, she accused him of infidelity.

His next film, *The Circus* (1928), was prepared under the cloud of this divorce, which was darkened by his mother's death. Charlie is chased into the center ring of a fourth-rate circus and becomes an instant hit with the audience. Yet he can be funny only by accident; when he is hired as a clown, he fails dismally. The critic Walter Kerr sees this as a core problem with the film. The premise—that comedy is created by accident—was not consistent with Chaplin's own beliefs. He worked extremely hard at his craft, constantly analyzing and expostulating the components of his comedy. He wrote about the humor of contrast and surprise, of a person made ridiculous who refuses to admit it, and of the natural desire to see a pompous person deflated.

By the time Chaplin was ready to make another picture, theaters were being wired for sound. He chose to make his next films silent, however, because he thought dialogue would destroy the character of the Tramp, interfere with the high art of pantomime, and hurt foreign sales. Nevertheless, he took advantage of the new technology to create sound effects, and he composed his own music and supervised the orchestration. Before this he had used published music and, from *The Kid* on, had indicated character themes on the cue sheets that were distributed with his films.

As a composer, Chaplin wrote "elegant and romantic music to frame my comedies in contrast to the Tramp character, for elegant music gave my comedies an emotional dimension." He had to hum his tunes to a professional arranger, because although he could play the piano and cello, he had never had a lesson and could not read music.

*City Lights* (1931), a silent film in the sound era, was a surprising financial success. Many critics also consider it among his greatest films. It is the love story of Chaplin's Tramp and a blind flower girl who believes he is rich. From a real millionaire, who befriends him in a drunken stupor, the Tramp gets money to pay for an operation to restore her sight. In the last, very poignant scene, which took months to shoot, the now well-to-do girl recognizes her benefactor by the feel of his hand. With a terrified smile, in a rare Chaplin close-up, he asks, "You can see now?" and she nods. The love story and the comedy of this film are completely intertwined. In one scene, as the Tramp sits near a fountain and moons over the blind flower girl, she comes to clean out her vase, throwing the rinse water right at him.

Partly to promote *City Lights*, but also because he thought a trip abroad might inspire him, Chaplin traveled around the world for fifteen months. He returned with an idea for a satire on mass production. *Modern Times* (1936) was another mainly silent film, but for the first time he wrote a screenplay. This film gave Chaplin a reputation as a radical. With those that followed, it was criticized for being too intellectual, although Chaplin insisted that "to entertain is my first consideration."

Several scenes in *Modern Times* are almost always praised, nevertheless. In one, a feeding machine is being tried out on Charlie as he continues to work on the assembly line. The device works properly until there is a short circuit. Then it dumps soup in his face and bolts

Charlie Chaplin with Virginia Cherrill in *City Lights*, United Artists, 1931. *Museum of Modern Art, Film Stills Archive.*

down his throat, carefully wiping his mouth afterward. In another scene, Chaplin has a nervous breakdown. With his two monkey wrenches, he attacks anything that looks like a screw, including the foreman's nose and the shiny black buttons on the front of a buxom woman's dress.

At the end of the film, Charlie typically walks down a lonely road into the sunset, but this time there is another homeless soul at his side, played by Paulette Goddard.

Chaplin had begun seeing the actress, twenty-two years his junior, in 1932. She struck him as "something of a *gamine* [a charming street child]. This would be a wonderful quality for me to get on the screen." He built a part in *Modern Times* around her. Chaplin and Goddard lived and traveled together—causing a scandal, since the date of their marriage is unclear—and seemed well suited. But after *The Great Dictator* (1940), in which she also appeared, they separated and were divorced.

*The Great Dictator,* Chaplin's first all-sound film, plays on the similarity in appearance between the Tramp and Hitler. In the film, a Jewish barber (Chaplin) ends up in a Tomanian army uniform and after a series of comic incidents is mistaken for Furor Adenoid Hynkel (also Chaplin). At the end the barber is speaking before a huge crowd who believe he is their dictator. His true love Hannah (Chaplin's mother's name), played by Goddard, listens to his serious and somewhat rambling words about humanity, democracy, and world peace. The six-minute speech drew criticism for being out of character and accounts for some of the mixed reviews. But, Chaplin asked, "May I not be excused for pleading for a better world?"

Chaplin's most controversial and least profitable film was the one that followed, *Monsieur Verdoux* (1947), about a Bluebeard-like character. A bank clerk with a crippled wife and young son loses his job. To support his family, he takes up as a profession the seduction and murder of elderly spinsters and leads a stylish second life. The film is an unsuccessful satire of modern business practices and a war-minded world. Verdoux, for instance, says to a reporter, "One murder makes a villain, millions a hero."

The 1940s were a hard time for Chaplin personally, and the bitterness in this film may reflect his lack of popularity in the United States. Because he had made speeches favoring a second front in World War II, to support Russia, he was accused of being a Communist and was even summoned before the House Un-American Activities Committee. The appearance was canceled, but he sent a letter saying, "I am not a Communist, neither have I ever joined any political party or organization in my life. I am what you call a peacemonger."

His personal life was also in the headlines again. First there was a tax evasion suit, which he eventually won. Then an actress with whom he was involved falsely accused him of having fathered her child. But all this misery had a happy ending, for in 1943, when he was fifty-four, Chaplin met and married Oona O'Neill, the eighteen-year-old daughter of the playwright Eugene O'Neill. They had eight children, and their marriage lasted until his death.

Chaplin's next screen effort was another essentially serious film, *Limelight* (1952). This movie is about a music-hall comedian named Calvero (Chaplin) who has lost his touch and is now an alcoholic living in a dingy apartment. The character is based on a real comedian, and also perhaps on Chaplin's father. Calvero nurses a hysterically paralyzed dancer to health, giving her the self-confidence to be a star. Later they meet again, and she arranges a benefit at which he performs with an accompanist (Buster Keaton). The show is a success, but Calvero dies at the end. Critics were lukewarm, some complaining that there was too much philosophizing.

When *Limelight* was done, the Chaplins decided to go to Europe. Aboard ship, he received a cable from the United States government stating that he could not return unless he answered charges "of a political nature and of moral turpitude." Instead of returning, they moved into a tiny village in Switzerland, where Chaplin spent the rest of his life.

He made two more films, neither of them very good. *A King in New York* (1957) is about a deposed and exiled king who agrees to do television commercials because he needs the money. He protects a young boy (played by Chaplin's son Michael), who runs away from school because he is tired of being asked if his parents are Communists. The film is obviously related to Chaplin's personal concerns, and he said later that it was "a little heavyhanded."

*A Countess from Hong Kong* (1967) is about a White Russian countess who stows away with the American ambassador on a ship bound from Hong Kong. There is a much overdone gag of the buzzer ringing in the cabin and their rushing to the other bedroom. The film got terrible reviews, and Chaplin had to admit that it was old-fashioned.

These late professional failures did not lessen the public's regard for Chaplin's genius. In 1971 he won a special award at the Cannes Film Festival; in 1972 he won an Oscar and made a victorious return to the United States; and in 1975 he was knighted by Queen Elizabeth. Chaplin filled his time at the end of his life by composing music for his silent films. But old age and its frailties began to creep up on him. He died in his sleep on December 25, 1977, in the midst of his family, who had gathered for their traditional Christmas celebration—a very different ending from any the Little Tramp had experienced.

# BUSTER
# KEATON

n America, Buster Keaton was known as the Great Stone Face. In France, he was called Malec (hole in a doughnut), and in other countries, Zephonio, Zybsko, Kazunk, Glo Glo, and Wong Wong—all meaning something like "zero" and referring to the blank face he presented to the screen. He explained his choice of the deadpan expression simply: "I just happened to be, even as a small kid . . . the type of comic that couldn't laugh at his own material. I soon learned at an awful early age that when I laughed the audience didn't."

Keaton first showed his face regularly on the vaudeville stage. Buster Keaton was born Jospeph Francis Keaton on October 4, 1895, in Piqua, Kansas. His parents, Myra and Joe Keaton, performed together in traveling medicine shows and later moved onto the fringes of vaudeville. His mother played the saxophone,

31

and his father was a natural comic and soft-shoe dancer. Joe Keaton was also famous for his high kick, which he used in his son's film *Our Hospitality* (1923) to knock off a man's hat.

According to legend, it was Harry Houdini, the Keatons' partner in the Mohawk Indian Medicine Company, who gave Buster his nickname when he was six months old. "Little Joe," as he was then known, fell down a flight of stairs and landed laughing. "That's some buster your baby took," Houdini commented, using stage jargon for a fall.

By the time Buster was four he was officially part of "The Three Keatons," one of the roughest knockabout comedy acts in vaudeville. An ad for the show read, "Maybe you think you were handled roughly when you were a kid—watch the way they handle Buster!" He was dressed as a comic Irishman, a miniature version of his father—with baggy pants, fancy vest, floppy shoes, a wig, and whiskers. His role, he said, was to "get in my father's way all the time and get kicked all over the stage."

Another brother and sister joined the act, but Buster was the star. As a result, his parents never sent him to school. Audiences accepted the violence of the act because he never seemed to be hurt (his expression never changed), but the Society for the Prevention of Cruelty to Children did not. Joe tried to spread a rumor that Buster was a midget, but finally the Keatons were banned from New York theaters and had to spend two years performing in England.

Over the next few years Joe Keaton drank more and more. His reflexes slowed, and he could be dangerously wild and rough. "When I smelled whisky across the stage, I got braced," Buster said. His father once kicked him so hard on the back of his neck that he remained unconscious for twenty-two hours. Some writers trace Keaton's later passivity with women and employers, and also the comic gloom of his great films, to these years of being abused on the stage. But Buster did not hold a grudge against his father and credited him with having taught him timing and how to make falls.

In 1917 Buster finally left the act. He was well known by then and quickly landed a role in a play. But before he could take it, he was introduced to the comedian Roscoe ("Fatty") Arbuckle, who invited him to act in *The Butcher Boy* (1917), the film he was then making for his Comique Film Corporation.

Although Joe Keaton had disdained the movies, Buster had already seen hundreds of the films that followed live performances in vaudeville theaters. From that first day with Arbuckle, he said, "I hadn't a doubt that I was going to love working in the movies."

During the next two years, from 1917 to 1919, Keaton made fifteen two-reelers and moved to California with the company. After three films he was made an assistant director, and his salary rose from $40 a week to $250. He and Arbuckle worked like partners, though Keaton's style and timing were more restrained than those of the former Mack Sennett comic. Arbuckle's scripts were never more than a few sentences and, according to Keaton, he "would turn you loose. Because he didn't care who got the laughs in his pictures. He wanted 'em in there."

Keaton was drafted near the end of World War I. (He had tried to enlist earlier but was turned down because he had flat feet and had lost part of his trigger finger in a clothes wringer as a child.) For about nine months he entertained troops in France with a snake dance and parodies of vaudeville stars.

On his return, Jack Warner and William Fox offered him four times the salary he had been getting at Comique, but Keaton remained loyal to Arbuckle and his producer Joseph Schenck. Arbuckle was the only teacher besides his father that he ever acknowledged. They were also good friends and spent hours together after work, drinking and playing practical jokes. Keaton supported Arbuckle during his notorious trial for rape and murder in 1922 and helped him to get jobs and money afterward.

Keaton also met his first wife at Comique. Natalie Talmadge, a sister of the famous actresses Norma and Constance, was a secretary and script girl for Arbuckle and occasionally played bit parts. She and Keaton were married in 1921.

By then Schenck had rented Arbuckle to Paramount to make features. He made Keaton the main star and director of Comique, taking over the Arbuckle unit and the best production team available. His salary was increased to $1,000, then $2,000, then $2,500 a week, and he got a quarter of the profits from his projects. What was most important, he had total freedom. Schenck, who by this time was managing all of Keaton's business affairs, got him his own lot and named it Keaton Studios. On his own, Keaton made nineteen two-reelers between 1920 and 1923 and ten features between 1923 and 1928, all considered masterpieces.

Keaton supervised every aspect of these films. In the early 1920s, he wrote, he and other comedians "worked with our writers from the day they started on a story. We checked on the scenery, the cast, the locations. . . . We directed our own pictures, making up our own gags as we went along, saw the rushes, supervised the cutting, cut to the sneak previews." The co-directors who appeared in the credits for his films during this time were really just assistants.

From the start, what most excited Keaton about filmmaking was "the way it automatically did away with the physical limitations of the theater. . . . In the theater you had to create an illusion of being on a ship, a railroad train, or an airplane. The camera allows you to show your audience the real thing."

Dangerous stunts were another mark of Keaton's devotion to realism. In *Sherlock, Jr.* (1924), he rode on the handlebars of a motorcycle with no driver; in *Our Hospitality* (1923), he went over a waterfall. One of his favorite stunts he tried out in two films before he perfected it in *Steamboat Bill, Jr.* (1928). In that film, the whole facade of a building falls down on top of him during a cyclone. Keaton remains upright, just fitting through an open window of the top floor. In planning this stunt, he allowed only a three-inch safety margin on each side.

Keaton performed all but one of his stunts himself, and he never cheated with camera tricks or cutting. In fact, he often used long takes to confirm that what was filmed was really happening. The only time he used a double was for *College* (1927), in which his character had to pole-vault into his sweetheart's room to rescue her.

Although he often portrayed a weakling, Keaton was a fine athlete who enjoyed pushing himself to the limit. The result, he once said, was that "I must have broken every bone of my body, one at a time." He risked drowning in almost every film he made, and in *Sherlock, Jr.* he broke his neck. Blinding headaches couldn't keep him away from work, however, and he didn't learn of the injury until an X-ray was taken years later.

Keaton preferred natural locations to the canvas sets on Hollywood lots, which most other comedians used. He had a passion for period details, and his two films set during the Civil War—*Our Hospitality* and *The General* (1926)—are among the most authentic-looking period films ever made in America.

Keaton loved tinkering. He once said that, given his choice, he would have been a civil engineer. In his Hollywood villa, he set up a miniature train to carry refereshments to guests. The mechanics of filmmaking also fascinated him. At Arbuckle's studio, "one of the first things I did was take a motion picture camera practically to pieces and find out the lenses and the splicing of film and how to get it on the projector."

As a director he was inspired by mechanical props. He once said, "The moment you give me a locomotive and things like that to play with, as a rule I find some way to get laughs out of it." Trains, in fact, appear in eight of his features. *The Navigator* (1924) was inspired by his discovery of an ocean liner that was about to be scrapped. Around it he built the story of a helpless,

Buster Keaton in *The Navigator,* Metro-Goldwyn, 1924. *Museum of Modern Art, Film Stills Archive.*

pampered young couple who are set adrift and must learn how to survive in their ungainly new home.

In some films he created complex machines to do simple tasks. *The Scarecrow* (1920) featured a mechanized house in which, as one title says, "all the rooms in this house are in one room." The sugar bowl and salt and pepper shakers hang from the ceiling on ropes. Pulleys deliver some foods from the refrigerator, and others arrive on a tiny electric train. The dinner table hangs on the wall, the bed becomes an organ, and the bathtub, turned on its side, becomes a sofa after the water spills into a duck pond.

Keaton also used ordinary machines in extraordinary ways. Faced with adapting a kitchen meant to serve a thousand to the needs of two, the young couple in *The Navigator* create a vast system of ropes, levers, and pulleys to set the table. A can opener made from a grindstone and a handsaw serves two purposes: it opens cans and it files Buster's nails. In *Cops* (1922), Buster, at the reins of a horse-drawn wagon, gets his hand bitten by a dog as he signals a turn. After that, he uses a boxing glove attached to a flexible tie rack as a turn signal. With this contraption, he casually punches a traffic cop twice at a busy intersection.

When Keaton began to make features, he abandoned the impossible cartoonlike gags that undermined the logic of the story. "I realized that my feature comedies would succeed best when the audience took the plot seriously enough to root for me as I indomitably worked my way out of mounting perils." While maintaining the dramatic integrity of his plot and the psychological integrity of his hero, Keaton managed to use the full range of traditional comedy, from low humor to comic irony.

One of his favorite comic techniques was visual surprise. Sometimes a message is partly obscured, changing its meaning. In *Seven Chances* (1925), Jimmie

Shannon (Keaton) must get married by 7:00 P.M. in order
to inherit $7 million. He sees what he thinks is a poster of
a sexy performer. He goes backstage to propose to her.
After he has left, movers take away a trunk from in front
of the poster, revealing that the performer is actually a
female impersonator.

Keaton often used visual surprises at the beginnings of his films. In *Cops* (1922), Buster seems to be
behind prison bars when actually he is outside the
garden gate of his sweetheart's estate. At the beginning
of *The Boat* (1921), Buster seems to be sailing on a storm-
tossed sea when actually he is being rocked by his son on
dry land.

The structure of Keaton's films is also a source of
laughter. They are often symmetrical, moving back and
forth, with endings neatly tied to beginnings. In *Seven
Chances*, first Jimmie is chasing potential brides; then
they are chasing him. In *The General*, an engineer (Keaton) first chases his stolen train north, then exactly re-
traces his route in his recaptured train as he is chased
back south.

Keaton used previews to "build up the high spots"
of his film. One of his greatest chase scenes was added
after a preview. In *Seven Chances*, he originally had
Jimmie running down a hill to escape the mob of women
who wanted to marry him. A few small rocks accidentally
broke loose and rolled after him. When Keaton heard the
audience's laughter at this, he had 150 more rocks spe-
cially built and used them in the additional scene.

Critics have often argued over who was the
greater comedian—Keaton or Chaplin. In the com-
parison, Keaton usually emerges as the greater filmmaker. Certainly he was aware of his medium and used it
deliberately. Several times he parodied popular films.
D. W. Griffith's serious three-part film *Intolerance* was
the inspiration for Keaton's first independent feature,

*The Three Ages* (1923). He sets the rivalry for the love of a beautiful girl in the Stone Age, Classical Rome, and modern times. The film begins with the Faithful Worshiper at Beauty's Shrine (Keaton) seated on a dinosaur and his rival (Wallace Beery) riding a mammoth.

*The Playhouse* (1921) was a technical triumph. "I kidded the habit of Tom Ince, an outstanding director, of giving himself every sort of screen credit possible on his pictures," Keaton said. The film is a minstrel show in which Keaton plays all the characters, including the audience. Using trick photography with multiple exposures, he is able to get nine Busters on the screen at the same time.

Keaton also stretched the limits of his films, creating striking sound gags in silent films and color gags in black-and-white movies. In *Our Hospitality*, Buster responds with a great start to the tray of silver that crashes to the floor behind him. In *Go West* (1925), he uses a red devil's tail to attract the attention of a herd of cattle.

His most obvious exploration of filmmaking, however, is in *Sherlock, Jr.* A movie projectionist (Keaton) falls asleep and dreams that he is involved with the characters on the screen. After he awakens, he still takes cues for romancing his sweetheart from the hero on the screen, checking back for further instructions after each step.

Keaton's features are basically one-man shows. Even his heroine is usually just a prop. He plays a variety of roles, and his character often changes or matures during the picture. But he usually enters as a small, solemn man alone in a world of apparently impossible odds. This character is different from Chaplin's Tramp. Only Friendless in *Go West*, the least typical of Keaton's heroes, comes close to the Tramp in evoking pathos. Keaton drew a different distinction between his character and Chaplin's. "Chaplin's tramp was a bum with a bum's philosophy," he said. "Lovable as he was he would steal if he got the chance. My little fellow was a working-man and honest."

Buster Keaton was a superb actor, not at all limited by the absence of expression on his character's face. "I had other ways of showing he was happy," he said. He communicated through actions, and his films had few subtitles.

Though Keaton's features made good profits, he did not do as well as Charlie Chaplin or Harold Lloyd. Keaton's films had high production costs, to which he never gave a thought. "If there is a costly way to make a movie," Schenck said, "he'll find it!" Keaton's films also had a quality that some viewers found disturbing. The critic James Agee said that "for those who sensed it, there was in his cinema a freezing whisper not of pathos but of melancholia." And Keaton himself, pathologically shy, could not engage the public personally like his gregarious contemporaries.

As his career flourished, Keaton's personal life deteriorated. His marriage was not happy, and after the birth of his second son, his wife ended their sexual relationship. Keaton retaliated by filling his evenings with bridge, baseball, and other women. Also, by the mid-1920s his social drinking had turned into alcoholism, though he could outdrink everyone else in the room and still appear sober.

In an attempt to improve his marriage, he gave Natalie the heroine's role in *Our Hospitality*, so that they could spend some time together on location. The gesture failed, but the film, based on the famous feud between the Hatfields and the McCoys, was one of Keaton's best. "I used a story of a feud in the South, and placed the period in 1831 to take advantage of the first railway train that had been built," Keaton said. He exactly reproduced that train for the film, as well as a fifteen-foot waterfall.

Willie McCay (Keaton), who was raised in the North, returns to the South to inherit his family's estate. On the train trip he meets and falls in love with Virginia (Natalie), from the rival family, who invites him to dinner. Since her father won't let his sons shoot Willie while he is their guest, much of the action revolves around their attempts to get him out of the house and his attempts to stay put. The humor is tied closely to the situation. Willie's dog, for instance, faithfully retrieves his hat each time he tries to hide it.

*The Navigator*, Keaton's next film, was his biggest moneymaker, after which Schenck gave him a new and much more generous contract. He did not want to have to worry about business, however, and unlike the shrewder Chaplin, he owned no shares in his own production company.

*The General*, Keaton's masterpiece, was his most expensive and least profitable film. It was based on a true story of northern spies during the Civil War who disguised themselves as southerners to steal a train called the *General* and take it to the North. It is also a successful transformation of history into a personal story with a real hero. Johnnie Gray (Keaton), the *General*'s engineer, recovers his train and his girl, then races south, destroying the train that is following him.

"I took that page of history," Keaton said, "and I stuck to it in all detail. I staged it exactly the way it happened." The *General* and the pursuing train, the *Texas*, were copied from originals, and it is a real train, not a model, that plunges when the bridge collapses at the end. Keaton went to Oregon to find the narrow-gauge railroad tracks he needed, bringing seventeen train cars full of equipment with him from Los Angeles.

In this film, too, the dramatic action and the comic business are closely meshed. At the end of the prologue

Buster Keaton with Marian Mack in *The General*, United Artists, 1926. *Museum of Modern Art, Film Stills Archive.*

Johnnie sits on the connecting bar between the *General*'s two biggest wheels, rising with it as the train starts to move. At the end, he is sitting there again, kissing Annabelle, while at the same time saluting passing soldiers with his free hand. The whole film, in fact, is structured so that almost everything that happens when Johnny is chasing the *General* recurs on his return.

Perhaps *The General* was too sophisticated for audiences of the time, with too much happening too fast. It got terrible reviews and was a financial disaster. Thus, after what is now considered one of the greatest films ever made, Keaton's creative freedom was threatened.

He made two more pictures independently. *College* is weak because the gags alone are better than the film as a whole. *Steamboat Bill, Jr.* has a common Keaton character, the effete young man who is changed by circumstances into a hero. Here Buster, the son of a rugged steamboat captain, arrives to visit his father after many years, wearing bell-bottoms, a polka-dot bow tie, and a beret, and carrying a ukulele. In the end, however, he courageously rescues his father from drowning.

In 1928, Keaton let Schenck talk him into giving up his own studio to work at MGM. Although he got three times his former salary, at MGM he was just an employee. He lost his old production staff, was prohibited from doing dangerous physical stunts, and was accountable for budgets and complete story scripts in advance. "The worst shock," he wrote, "was discovering I could not work up stories the way I'd been doing, starting only with the germ of an idea." The results were mostly undistinguished.

Keaton's alcoholism grew worse. In 1932, his wife finally left him, taking almost everything he had, including his two sons. When she changed their name to Talmadge, Keaton's response was typically passive. He explained in his autobiography that they were probably better off being in line to inherit the Talmadge riches. But he drank himself to sleep at night and drank to keep himself going during the day. MGM sent him to several expensive sanitariums, then fired him.

After that came a series of professional and personal disasters, including a brief second marriage to a gold-digging sanitarium nurse. Keaton called the years 1933 to 1935 "the two worst years of my life." He supported himself by making two-reelers and some cheap feature films outside the United States. Finally, in 1937, he took a job as a gag writer at MGM.

His life "started on the upgrade" again in 1940. He

had sobered up by then and that year married Eleanor Norris, a contract dancer at MGM. Though she was twenty-four years his junior, their marriage was happy, and he was able to reestablish contact with his sons. In the 1950s he began to appear on television and got some cameo roles in films. The most famous of these was his improvised part in *Limelight* (1952). He plays a near-sighted pianist who accompanies Charlie Chaplin in his comeback as a music-hall comedian.

Keaton was rediscovered by film critics in the late 1950s, and during the 1960s there were very successful retrospectives of his films at the Cinémathèque Française and the Venice Film Festival. Keaton was typically modest. "I never realized I was doing anything but trying to make people laugh when I threw my custard pies and took pratfalls," he said. He didn't have long to enjoy his newfound renown, however, for he died of lung cancer on February 1, 1966.

The summary of his life Keaton wrote in his autobiography has the same "freezing whisper of melancholia" as many of his films. "I think I had the happiest and luckiest of lives. Maybe this is because I never expected as much as I got . . . and when the knockers came I felt it was no surprise. I had always known life was like that, full of uppercuts for the deserving and undeserving alike."

# JOHN FORD

hen I pass on," John Ford said in 1971, "I want to be remembered as 'John Ford—a guy that made Westerns.'" As usual, Ford was dismissing the critics who call him an artist and his films art. Yet some of the best of the more than 135 films Ford directed during his half-century in Hollywood are not Westerns, and his Westerns are not simple shoot-'em-ups. Ford's films tend to revolve around the themes of community, family, traditional values, sacrifice, and defeat. Their subjects range from war and action to history and Americana; and they include Irish stories and others that fit no category.

Over the years Ford's reputation has risen and fallen. He has been criticized for sentimentality, American chauvinism, and broad humor, and critics disagree about his later films especially. Yet his pictorial sense and his gift for storytelling and myth-making are generally acknowledged. "John Ford knows what the earth is made of," Orson Welles said of his favorite director.

Ford brought with him to Hollywood his Irish-American background—a rebelliousness, a lyricism, and a feeling for religion and family. His commitment to Ireland remained so strong, in fact, that he left his wife and his Hollywood bosses to join the fight against the British Army in 1921. He spent six months in Ireland, although he probably never actually fired a gun.

John Ford was born Sean Aloysius O'Feeney on February 1, 1895, the last of eleven children, only six of whom survived. He grew up near Portland, Maine, where his father, a farmer and later a saloon owner, had settled more than twenty years earlier.

John spent much of his childhood looking out toward the sea and dreaming of becoming a sailor. When he wasn't accepted by the Naval Academy at Annapolis, he enrolled at the University of Maine, where he had an athletic scholarship. But he lasted there only three weeks. Then he took off for Hollywood, where his brother Francis was acting in and directing Westerns.

Ford was rejected by the navy again, during World War I, because of his poor eyesight (he was very nearsighted and could see only a blur without thick glasses). But he managed to satisfy his patriotic impulses by creating almost a second career in the Naval Reserve, retiring as a rear admiral. During the 1930s, he used his own yacht to spy on suspected Japanese and German agents off the coasts of California and Mexico. He also spent three and a half years during World War II and eight months of the Korean War as head of the Field Photographic Branch of the Office of Strategic Services, the predecessor of the CIA. His fifteen film crews were responsible for aerial reconnaissance and made training films and documentaries.

On arriving in Hollywood, he took the last name Ford, as his brother had, and worked as Francis's stuntman and general assistant. He was soon put in charge of groups of extras and cowboys, and by 1917, at the age of twenty-two, he had a contract with Universal as a director. Ford was hired to work with their Western star Harry Carey, with whom he made twenty-six films.

He and Carey wrote rough scripts together, and by working twelve hours a day, seven days a week, they could finish a two-reeler in five or six days and a feature in six weeks. They had no time for rehearsals. But even later in his career, Ford preferred not to rehearse action sequences or emotional scenes for fear that the actors would lose their spontaneity.

Most of his films with Carey had conventional Western plots revolving around corrupt sheriffs, family feuds, range wars, or a hero's search for his father's murderers. Many of the negatives were destroyed in a studio fire and cannot be seen today. But contemporary reviewers praised their visual style. Ford saw them as "character stories" and tried to make them historically accurate. There was no "so-called quick-draw stuff, nobody wore fancy clothes and we didn't have dance hall scenes with girls in short dresses." Carey played "a saddle tramp, instead of a great bold gun-fighting hero." He was often a loner, in trouble with the law, who was drawn into a fight for social justice.

Ford's working style developed during these early years in Hollywood. He used over and over the same group of actors and technicians, shot quickly, and preferred to film on location, even if that meant braving heat, cold, or storms. He paid no attention to how he looked on the set. He wore baggy pants and an old cap and always had either a cigar or the end of his handkerchief in his mouth. He also probably started drinking heavily at this time. Toward the end of his career, he had binges lasting several days.

By 1920 Ford had a reputation as a top action director and was able to double his salary by switching from Universal to Fox. That year, also, he met his wife, Mary McBride Smith, a beautiful young woman with money and background and even family connections to the navy. Although they had two children, and the marriage lasted throughout Ford's lifetime, it was strained by his infidelity and his occasional disappearances for drunken adventures with his male friends.

In his ten years at Fox, Ford had less freedom than before. He was forced to accept assignments and to broaden his range beyond Westerns. Although he scorned the producers, he took pride and pleasure in being able to direct whatever was given to him. "I like to be on the set," he said, "and regardless of what the story is, I like to work in pictures." He was now an experienced director, called "Pappy" before he was thirty by casts and crews. During his years at Fox, Ford also established himself as a director of talkies, though he claimed he was a man of the silent camera. "That's when pictures and not words had to tell the story."

Ford worked in varying degrees of collaboration with writers, but he alone determined camera angles, and he was known for replacing wordy speeches with eloquent silences. The original script of *The Informer* (1935), for instance, contained a long interchange in which British officers paid off the Irish informer. Ford reduced it to a silent scene in which the money is pushed across the table with a cane and the only words are "Twenty pounds. You'd better count it. Go out the back way." On the other hand, two screenwriters have praised Ford's ear for dialogue and credit him with having written the best lines in their films. In *The Quiet Man* (1952) he gave a rural Irish character this line: "It's a fine, soft night so I think I'll go and talk a little treason with my comrades."

Ford also used his sound track dramatically. He chose evocative popular tunes for background: "Red River Valley" in *The Grapes of Wrath* (1940), "The Isle of Innisfree" in *The Quiet Man*, and the title songs in *She Wore a Yellow Ribbon* (1949) and *My Darling Clementine* (1946). And a very effective scene in *Two Rode Together* (1961) was shot and recorded in the middle of a river so that the conversation of the two men is punctuated by the real sound of gurgling water.

Ford's best and most successful films during his time at Fox were not the assignments but the few projects he chose himself, such as *The Iron Horse* (1924). This story of a son's search for his father's murderer, set against the background of the building of America's first transcontinental railroad, was Ford's earliest major box office success. As always, he took advantage of accidents and incorporated into the script the three blizzards the company encountered on location. The film also contains several Ford trademarks: Indians appearing on a ridge, riders disappearing into the sunset, and a combination of action and humor.

It was also at Fox that Ford began his collaboration with Dudley Nichols, a screenwriter with artistic ambitions. They worked together on and off through the 1930s and early 1940s. Their most famous project was *The Informer*, the film that first brought Ford serious critical attention. *The Informer*, based on a novel by Liam O'Flaherty, is set in Dublin during the Irish Rebellion, which Ford had experienced firsthand. It is about Gypo Nolan, a poor, brutish, pitiful man who for twenty pounds leads the British to his friend, a leader of the rebellious Irish Republican Army. With his usual concern for the victim and the outlaw, Ford presented this character sympathetically.

He shot the film in a deliberately artistic style, as he did other films he made with Nichols, using some of the sophisticated design and lighting techniques he had observed in Germany several years earlier. Usually, however, photographic style is not overemphasized in Ford's films. "I try to make people forget they're in a theater," he said. "I want them to feel that what they're seeing is real." The swirls of mist and the symbols (a "Wanted" poster for Gypo's friend follows the informer around) now seem heavy-handed. Yet the film was a critical and financial success and won four Academy Awards, including Ford's first for direction.

What is still impressive about the film is the performance that Ford wrenched from Victor McLaglen (Gypo), one of his regulars, who had never before played a role with such a wide emotional range. At times Ford secretly filmed what McLaglen thought were just rehearsals, and the night before shooting the scene of Gypo's trial by an IRA court, Ford encouraged McLaglen to go out drinking. His hangover the next morning contributed to the confusion and pain the character shows on the screen.

John Ford was known for being able to evoke fine, natural performances. This was partly a result of working often with the same actors, whose personalities he knew and could use. He also created with his real-life cast and crew the very feeling of community and family loyalty he wanted his films to express. On location there was always a camplike atmosphere with entertainment planned every night.

According to Anna Lee (*Fort Apache, How Green Was My Valley*), Ford had a "clairvoyance, an almost mystical way of manipulating your emotions. . . . He could put you in almost any state of mind he wanted to." Maureen O'Hara (*Rio Grande, The Quiet Man*), said, "he seems to know just what's necessary to get a good performance from anyone; some people he'll be entirely gentle with, and with others he'll be a brute." Ford created tension on the set by choosing a scapegoat. John Wayne, who endured the worst of his baiting, was ultimately closest to the director.

With Ford, there was little discussion of the script or of the characters' motivations. But according to Henry Fonda, "He somehow gave you a piece of business or something that made the scene—there was only one way to play it." One of these is the whimsical little dance Fonda does as Wyatt Earp in *My Darling Clementine*, shifting his feet against the porch post as he leans back in his chair.

After 1931, Ford was well enough regarded not to need the exclusive contract with Fox. For the next several years he alternated studio assignments with projects of his own like *The Informer*, with themes that interested him. But even in his studio assignments he had more control over everything—from casting to prop details to cutting—than did most directors.

He earned his freedom partly by making films that did well at the box office and partly by being a thorough professional. He shot fast and used little film, finishing early and under budget. Ford worked on instinct. He never planned out sequences of shots on paper, but he was usually able to get what he wanted on the first take. He also took no guff from his producers. The story is told of Ford introducing one of them to his cast and crew. "Now, get a good look at this guy," he said. "He is the producer. Look at him now, because you will not see him again on this set until the picture is finished."

After his stretch of independence, Ford returned to 20th Century Fox to make some of his best films. Many critics consider the years from 1939 to 1946, from *Stagecoach* to *My Darling Clementine*, his artistic peak. The films of this period tend to focus on common people

Henry Fonda in *My Darling Clementine*, 20th Century Fox, 1946.
*Museum of Modern Art, Film Stills Archive.*

who become heroes in special situations. Ford talked of a "tragic moment," which makes "individuals aware of each other by bringing them face-to-face with something bigger than themselves" and "forces men to reveal themselves and to become aware of what they truly are."

*Stagecoach* (1939) is filled with the outcasts who interested Ford. The passengers traveling together through Apache territory in the 1880s include a prostitute, a convict (the Ringo Kid, played by John Wayne in his first romantic lead), a drunken doctor, a gambler, a whiskey salesman, and a crooked banker. The first three, thrown out of town by the self-righteous Ladies' Law and Order League, show their heroism during the birth of a baby and a terrifying chase by Indians.

Even in a film with so much action, Ford kept his camera fairly still. The movement comes from following the stagecoach. "To me the camera is an information booth," Ford said. "I like to keep it still and have the characters come to it and tell their story."

Ford's first Western in thirteen years was a critical and commercial success. Some viewers now see it as contrived, and its characters—the prostitute with the heart of gold, the good badman—seem like clichés because they have been borrowed so often for Westerns since. But the critic Andrew Sarris, who called Ford "one of the foremost poets of the screen," wrote of *Stagecoach* that "what makes Ford's characters unique in the Western Epic is [the] double image, alternating between close-ups of emotional intimacy and long shots of epic involvement, thus capturing both the twitches of life and the silhouettes of legend."

The Indians in this film are slaughtered, but the killing is not dwelt upon. Here as elsewhere, Ford shows their courage and dignity. He often silhouetted groups of Indians in a long shot against the horizon. Visually, they are part of the landscape and the whites are the intruders. In real life, also, he tried to be fair to the Indians. *Stagecoach* was the first of nine films Ford shot in Monument Valley, an isolated area of great natural drama near the Utah state line in the Navajo reservation. Ford insisted on paying the Indians who worked for him the full Hollywood wage.

In contrast to *Stagecoach*, Ford's next fim and his favorite, *Young Mr. Lincoln* (1939), has very little action. Its point of highest drama is a courtroom scene in which Lincoln (played by Henry Fonda) defends two young men wrongly accused of murder and gets the real murderer to confess. The idea of the picture, according to Ford, was "to give the feeling that even as a young man you could sense there was going to be something great about this man." Abe naturally assumes the role of mediator. As the judge of a pie-baking contest, he keeps tasting the last two pies but never picks a winner.

While this film focuses on the common humanity of an American hero, Ford's next film, *The Grapes of Wrath* (1940), also starring Fonda, shows the heroism of common people. The Joads have been thrown off their tenant farm in Oklahoma. They bundle their possessions onto a wagon and head west, attracted by the false promise of fruit-picking jobs and good wages in California. The family is held together through many trials only by the strength of Ma Joad. Although the upbeat ending is untrue to Steinbeck's novel, the sufferings of these realistically portrayed characters are movingly conveyed.

*How Green Was My Valley* (1941) emphasizes the importance of family through the disintegration of one family. The Morgans, a Welsh mining family, and the community they live in are broken up by economic conditions. The sons leave to find work elsewhere, and the father is killed in a mine cave-in. This film won six Oscars, including one for direction, more than any other

Ford film. Ford also said it was his happiest film because the cast became like a family.

Then, at the height of his career, Ford took off to serve with the Field Photographic Branch in World War II. As a military assignment he made *They Were Expendable* (1945), about America's loss of the Philippines after the bombing of Pearl Harbor.

When the war was over, Ford turned back to the Western with *My Darling Clementine* (1946), a film about Wyatt Earp and Doc Holliday, and their legendary gunfight at the O.K. Corral with the villainous Clantons. More important than history, however, is the theme again of family. Graveside visits are a common ritual in Ford films. Lincoln visits the grave of his first love, Ann Rutledge, for instance, when he is trying to decide whether to become a lawyer. In *Clementine*, Wyatt pledges at the grave of his youngest brother, who was murdered by the Clantons, to "make a country where kids like you can grow up safe."

Ford shows Wyatt Earp, like Lincoln, as both a legend and a man. When the Clantons hear that he is to be the new marshal of Tombstone, they laugh—until he tells them his name. On the other hand, he can be the simple country boy dancing with Clementine or rocking back in his chair on the porch.

After this film, Ford and the producer Merian C. Cooper set up their own production company, Argosy, which lasted from the late 1940s to the early 1950s. Their first film, *The Fugitive* (1947), about a martyred priest, was based on *The Power and the Glory* by Graham Greene. Its screenplay by Dudley Nichols, their last collaboration, was overly symbolic, and the film failed with both the critics and the public. Ford has been criticized for shooting the Argosy films too hastily, without his usual care.

Among those that stand out are the Westerns that

make up Ford's Cavalry Trilogy: *Fort Apache* (1948), *She Wore a Yellow Ribbon* (1949), and *Rio Grande* (1950). In these films the seventh United States Cavalry replaces the individual in its devotion to duty, honor, and civilization and is also explored as a community in itself. In all three, John Wayne plays the ideal cavalryman, always putting his company first.

Ford's favorite of the three was *She Wore a Yellow Ribbon*. He said that he tried to give it the color and movement of the western paintings of Frederic Remington. It is the story of the last mission of Captain Nathan Brittles before his retirement from the cavalry after forty-three years. Wayne described one of the effective bits of business Ford added to a scene in which the men of Brittles's company give him a silver watch with an inscription as a retirement gift: "He had me reach for an old pair of bifocals. I'm embarrassed and fumble with them. It was a bit of comedy that perfectly balanced the sentiment and kept the scene from becoming maudlin."

Ford's favorite of all his Westerns, however, was *Wagonmaster* (1950), for which he wrote the original story. It is about a wagon train of Mormon pioneers making their way west in the 1880s. It honors the decency and humanity of this community of outsiders. The Mormons prove their tolerance by accepting a troupe of medicine show people who ask to join them. Later on, the Mormons show their courage by standing up to a family of outlaws.

A non-Western film that Ford had long wanted to make was *The Quiet Man*, which he shot on location in County Galway, Ireland, his parents' birthplace. This was his first successful romantic love story and his only film to be just that. In it he paired John Wayne and Maureen O'Hara, who had first played together in *Rio Grande*. It is the story of an American ex-boxer who has sworn off using his fists after killing an opponent in the

John Ford with Maureen O'Hara and John Wayne on location for *Rio Grande*, Republic, 1950. *Museum of Modern Art, Film Stills Archive.*

ring. He goes to his mother's homeland in search of simplicity and innocence. There his courtship of a country girl is filled with humorous mishaps until he accepts the community's conventions and earns his bride by fighting her brother. This warm, pretty film was one of the great popular successes of Ford's career and won him the last of his six Oscars.

Movies were becoming harder to put together, however, because the industry was suffering from the breakup of the distribution system and the growing popularity of television. Ford himself had less energy and enthusiasm. In 1953 he had cataracts removed from both eyes. His right eye became light-sensitive and useless for reading, and he had to wear a patch over it.

His last seventeen films are of uneven quality, and this period is seen in general as one of decline rather than maturity. Several films, however, have strong critical supporters: *The Searchers* (1956), a Western and, according to Ford, "the tragedy of a loner who could never really be part of the family"; *Sergeant Rutledge* (1960), about a black soldier of the Ninth Cavalry falsely accused of rape; *The Man Who Shot Liberty Valance* (1962), Ford's saddest and most pessimistic Western, about the closing of the frontier and the end of the Old West; *Cheyenne Autumn* (1964), a Western told from the Indians' point of view; and *Seven Women* (1966), his last film, about missionaries in China in 1935.

*The Searchers* is the most famous of these, and some critics call it Ford's masterpiece. The film begins and ends with a common Ford image—the hero in a frame within a frame. The house door opens to reveal the solitary figure of Ethan Edwards (John Wayne), and the same door closes on him at the end. After Ethan leaves his brother's family, Comanches raid the house, killing everyone except one daughter, whom they take with them. Ethan and her foster brother search for her for five years only to find that she has become a squaw. With his violence and racism, Ethan is a disturbing hero, very different from the men of good will who are usually the heroes of Ford's films. But the film is identifiably Ford's. It has his vast aerial views and an epic quality. Its mood is just much darker than ever before.

At the age of seventy-one, John Ford finally stopped making movies. He became more and more reclusive. In 1971 he was diagnosed as having cancer, though he never discussed his disease. At a ceremony in 1973 he was given the Life Achievement Award by the American Film Institute and the Medal of Freedom, the highest civilian award, by the President of the United States. Five months later on August 31, 1973, he died in his sleep.

# FRANK CAPRA

aybe there really wasn't an America," the filmmaker John Cassavetes said, "maybe it was only Frank Capra." In his best films during the 1930s and 1940s, Capra was able to humanize on the screen the ideal of the American character. His films showed ordinary people from small towns triumphing over evil and powerful forces by doing what was right and sensible. "Let others make films about the grand sweeps of history. I'd make mine about the bloke that pushes the broom," he wrote in his autobiography.

Capra also wrote that films were his "way of saying, 'Thanks, America,'" to the country that had adopted him and fostered his climb from poverty to prosperity. Frank Capra was born on May 18, 1897, the sixth of seven children of poor Italian farmers. When he was six, the family immigrated to Los Angeles, where his father got a job as a farmhand and his mother worked in an olive oil plant. All the children were expected to help support the family. Frank delivered newspapers, worked as a janitor at school, and played the guitar at night in a cabaret.

In his determination not to remain poor, Frank focused on education as the escape route. Against his family's wishes, he enrolled at the California Institute of Technology, paying his way as well as his share of family expenses with scholarships and odd jobs. In the spring of 1918 he graduated with a B.S. in chemical engineering.

Instead of taking a job immediately, he enlisted in the army. But when the war was over, there were no jobs for engineers. Capra returned home depressed and suffering from severe stomach pains, which lasted for over a year. His mother couldn't afford a doctor at the time, and not until fifteen years later did he discover that his appendix had burst.

Capra spent the next three years "on the 'bum' "— wandering throughout the western United States, doing everything from picking fruit to peddling photographs from door to door. From these experiences, he said, he "got a real sense of small towns, got a real sense of America," and "fell in love" with his country.

That Frank Capra became a filmmaker was pure chance. Back again in Los Angeles, he read in the newspaper that a former Shakespearean actor was opening a studio to make films from poems. With his con man's skills still fresh from the road, he introduced himself as a man "from Hollywood" and was immediately hired to direct Rudyard Kipling's melodramatic "Ballad of Fultah Fisher's Boarding House." Although he had never been interested in movies, he discovered he had an intuitive talent for handling the camera, and he found that he liked it. The first time he looked through the camera, "I got a terrific thrill, goose pimples ran up and down my back."

Capra realized that he had much to learn before he could be a "Hollywood director."He decided to begin his education in a film laboratory. He processed film and spliced and edited newsreels and advertising films. He then got a job as a property man and finally as a gag writer for slapstick comedies. In 1924 Mack Sennett hired him to work with a new comedian named Harry Langdon. Capra helped shape Langdon's character into what he called the "little elf," who *"trusted* his way through adversities, surviving only with the help of God, or goodness."

Langdon left Sennett to make a feature for First National, taking Capra along as writer and director. Although Langdon's little elf was simpler than the typical Capra hero, Capra used in their two films together some of the same themes that he would use in his own films later—the love of small towns and fear of big cities, and the immoral enemy. He also discovered his inclination for comedy and developed his skill for visual humor. But the two men soon disagreed about the character they were creating, and Langdon fired Capra, denying publicly that Capra had directed him. Ironically, although Capra had trouble finding another job, Langdon's character lost focus and his career never recovered.

The year 1927 was another low for Capra. He was out of work, and his two-year marriage to an actress had suffered irremediably from his long working days and her drinking. He directed one comedy for First National, which was a commercial failure, and had to go back to Sennett.

Soon, however, he was to meet two people who would change his luck and his life. One was Harry Cohn, production chief of a minor studio, Columbia Pictures, which Capra would raise to prominence and with which he would be associated for thirteen years. The other was Lucille Reyburn, who would become his wife and the mother of his children and with whom, he wrote in his autobiography, he was still having a romance thirty-eight years later.

In 1928, Cohn offered Capra a job, and Capra accepted—on his own terms. Although his starting salary was only $1,000 a film, he controlled all the writing, directing, producing, and editing. Some scripts he chose from story properties owned by Columbia; others he asked the studio to buy; and still others he wrote himself.

Capra always worked closely with his writers and then improvised at times while shooting. He also shot more film than he needed so that he could select, cut, and rearrange it in the cutting room, where he was constantly present. He considered editing "the greatest fun about filmmaking," and it was an important component of his style. Capra later called this involvement in every aspect of his films the "one man, one film" principle.

Capra directed fifteen feature films for Columbia in less than four years. They were made inexpensively and quickly (two weeks to write, two weeks to shoot, two weeks to edit). In them he tried out different genres and subjects and experimented with camera techniques. "Mastering the language of film," he wrote, was "not just a desire—it had become an obsession."

In these films, also, he began to focus on certain themes and to develop his own style. *That Certain Thing* (1928), for instance, his first Columbia film, is about a gold digger who marries a rich heir. When he is cut off from his inheritance, however, she discovers that she is really in love with him. Capra showed his distaste for greedy capitalists and his faith in the ability of his characters to overcome class differences.

To *Submarine* (1928), a melodrama about two sailors in love with the same girl, he added new elements of visual realism. For this film, which he took over from another director, Capra insisted that the leads remove their makeup, and he gave them wrinkled uniforms and licorice to chew like tobacco. This was a silent film with sound effects added later, but Capra had no trouble making the transition to sound. "I wasn't at home in silent films," he said. "I thought it was very strange to stop and put a title on the screen and then come back to the action."

As early as 1929 Capra described his style as "comedy in all things. Laughter was the disarmer. The friendmaker. Entertain them, and audiences would accept most anything." His frequent screenwriter Robert Riskin helped him to accomplish this. The two became good friends and collaborated on most of Capra's important films during the Depression years. Their intimate collaboration, according to Capra, was one of "sparking and building on each other's ideas. . . . In general I stayed ahead of him, thinking up the next batch of scenes which, when agreed upon, he would put into dialogue form." Capra noted, however, that he was always the one to give the final yes or no.

Their *American Madness* (1932) was one of the first films to deal directly with the Depression. An idealistic banker (Walter Huston) is faced with a panic caused by the rumor of a robbery. To show the rumor spreading, Capra used a montage of about fifty shots. He also added a sense of urgency by speeding up the pace of the film by one-third, a technique he continued to use. He hurried the actors, cut out long walks and dissolves, and allowed speeches to interrupt and overlap, as they do in real life.

In this film, as in others, Capra expresses his fear of even the best people acting as a mob. George Bailey, in *It's a Wonderful Life* (1947), stops the run at his Building and Loan by breaking down the mob into individuals, confronting his customers one by one.

Capra cast the crowd scenes in *American Madness* himself. "I like to fill the screen with people—I love faces," he said. He made them convincing by giving each bit player a specific identity, an only daughter, for instance, worried about her sick mother. This would "fix her mood, her thinking, her attitude, and audiences will sense her as a real person, not an actress."

Capra was known for getting strong, natural performances from actors. His technique, he said, was to watch the actor's interpretation of a role before he gave his own. "I want to find out what he thinks before I start to tell him what I think." He also always gave his actors something to do. In *Mr. Deeds Goes to Town* (1936), for instance, Jean Arthur spins a yo yo, and the judge at Deeds's trial drums his fingers. "You don't just set actors up and let them talk; you give them 'business' to do while they're yakking." Perhaps most important, Capra's set, according to Jean Arthur, was one of "great warmth and protection."

*It Happened One Night* (1934) may be Capra's best-loved film. A newspaper reporter who has quit his job (Clark Gable) and a runaway heiress (Claudette Colbert) meet on a long bus ride. After instant and mutual dislike, they begin to shed their preconceptions about each other, and finally fall in love. In one scene, he introduces her to the simple pleasure of coffee and doughnuts: "Twenty million dollars and you don't know how to dunk?" he muses.

Another particularly effective scene was improvised. A hillbilly duet is rehearsing on the bus. Capra told the "passengers" to join in when they felt like it and told the stars to slowly warm up to each other. He considered such loose, musical scenes important for a film and used them often. "When the audience rests and

Frank Capra with Claudette Colbert and Clark Gable on set of *It Happened One Night*, Columbia, 1934. *Museum of Modern Art, Film Stills Archive.*

they look at the people," he said, "they begin to smile. They begin to love the characters, and *then* they'll be worried about what happens to them. If the audience doesn't like your people, they won't laugh at them and they won't cry with them."

This film, which is considered the first "screwball comedy," won all the major Academy Awards for 1934. Instead of reveling in his success, however, Capra was overwhelmed by a fear that he wouldn't be able to do it again. He first pretended to be sick and then really got sick, losing more than thirty pounds and running a constant high fever. Finally a friend sent someone (described in Capra's autobiography as "the little man") to visit him. This nameless man accused Capra of throwing away his talents when he could have been doing good in a troubled world, and challenged him to recover.

Capra now had a purpose to his work beyond personal ambition: to "lift the human spirit." "My films had to *say* something. And whatever they said had to come from those ideas inside me 'that were hurting to come out.' From then on, my scripts would take from six months to a year to write and rewrite; to carefully—and subtly—integrate ideals and entertainment into a meaningful tale."

Some critics, like Alistair Cooke, complained that "he's started to make movies about themes instead of people." Yet the late 1930s were the years of Capra's greatest success and prestige as a director. From 1935 to 1939, years of labor organizing, he was president of the Motion Picture Academy, and from 1938 to 1939 he was president of the Screen Directors Guild, fighting to keep it alive. The five films he made between 1938 and 1941 were nominated for thirty-one Oscars and won six. At a time when people went to the movies to see stars, Frank Capra was a star director, his name appearing above the titles of his films after 1936.

Capra's films have been given every label from Communist to conservative. Yet his vantage point is moral rather than political. He presents the political system in his films as basically good except for a few rotten apples—greedy capitalists, crooked politicians, and intellectual snobs. Capra focuses on the emotional and moral issues his characters face and on their relationships.

Capra's hero is the common man who embodies our best national traits—honor, common sense, lack of pretension, idealism, devotion to family and country. Longfellow Deeds of Mandrake Falls (*Mr. Deeds Goes to Town*) is one. He is uninterested in the large inheritance left to him and ignores the slick lawyers who first tell him of his new fortune. In one of the most famous moments in Capra's films, as the train is about to pull out from Mandrake Falls, the frantic lawyers find the heir in the farewell crowd, playing the bass part of "Auld Lang Syne" on his tuba. Once in the big city, Mr. Deeds outwits the sycophants who try to dig into his pockets and finally works out a scheme to give all his money away so that he can go back home.

Typically, he also wins the heart of a cynical newspaper reporter, Babe Bennett (Jean Arthur), who sets out to write stories that make fun of the Cinderella Man, as she calls him. The danger in a film like this, as Capra well knew, is that the main character's sincerity will become maudlin and result in what some critics called "Capra-corn." To avoid this, Capra lets Deeds read Babe one of his doggerel love poems, then releases the laugh purposely by having him fall over a garbage can.

In choosing Gary Cooper to play Deeds, holding up production for months until he was free, Capra was following his usual method of casting: using actors whose personalities were most like those of the characters and then encouraging them to play themselves. Of Cooper he said, "He's simple, but he's strong and honest, and there's integrity written all over him."

For the lead in *Mr. Smith Goes to Washington* (1939), Capra chose James Stewart: "He has a look of an intellectual about him. And he can be an idealist." Stewart plays Jefferson Smith, head of the Boy Rangers, who is chosen by machine politicians to fill an empty senatorial seat because of his political innocence. He is contrasted with the state's other senator, Paine (Claude Rains), who has already been compromised. "This is a man's world, a brutal world," Paine tells him, "and you've got to check your ideals at the door." Jean Arthur, whom Capra described as "a tough gal with a heart of gold," plays Smith's aide Saunders, another cynic to be converted.

This film illustrates Capra's great technical skill and painstakingly realistic sets. Here he used the proper Senate procedures and exactly reproduced even such tiny details as a hole kicked in Jefferson Davis's desk by a Union soldier. He also used a variety of editing techniques. Smith's patriotic tour of the capital is a breathtaking montage of national monuments. During the endless filibuster the young senator stages to stall the machine politicians' plans and recruit support from his state, Capra cuts back and forth between the huge politically controlled newspaper and the Boy Rangers' tiny "Boys' Stuff" operation. He also uses reaction shots—of the press corps, of Saunders prompting from the gallery, and of the senators on the floor grumbling—to add to the drama.

As usual, Capra previewed the film before completing it and recorded the response. He then re-edited, often allowing more time between gag lines. He also previewed several different endings. Audiences chose the ambiguous one he used, in which Smith wins the filibuster and Paine confesses, but the machine is not totally destroyed.

After this film, Capra joined Riskin to form Frank Capra Productions. This company lasted only a year and a half because of high tax costs, but long enough to produce *Meet John Doe* (1941). This is the darkest of Capra's films, with the most evil villain and a hero who almost jumps off a building.

A reporter (Barbara Stanwyck) writes a fake letter, signed "John Doe," complaining about the state of society and threatening to commit suicide. When it creates a huge outpouring of support, her publisher decides to exploit it for his own political ends (he believes that "what the American people need is an iron hand"). He hires Long John Willoughby (Gary Cooper), an unemployed baseball player, to play John Doe. Soon people are organizing John Doe clubs around the theme "Love thy neighbor." When Willoughby begins to believe in his mission and rebels against his boss, the publisher exposes him and his disillusioned followers desert.

In this film Capra perfected his "reactive character," another technique he used to prevent his films from becoming overly sentimental. Jean Arthur, as Saunders or Bennett, sometimes served as a reactive character, but in *John Doe* the character is the Colonel (Walter Brennan), Willoughby's sidekick from his hobo days. When Long John says that he hopes neighbors will tear down the fences between them, the Colonel laughs. "Tear down all the fences?" he says. "Why, if you tear down one picket of your neighbor's fence he'd sue ya."

Partly because Willoughby does not fit the mold of the ideal American character, Capra couldn't find a satisfactory ending for the film. He shot four different ones to be shown to preview audiences, then chose a fifth recommended by a viewer: the John Doe club members beg their former hero not to jump to his death. But Capra admitted himself that "*still* it was a letdown."

For three and a half years during World War II Capra served in the Army Pictorial Service. He was awarded the Distinguished Service Medal for producing a series of training films called "Why We Fight." The first of these, *Prelude to War* (1942), also won an Academy Award as Best Documentary.

The raw material of these films was newsreels, official Allied films, and captured enemy films. They were edited together to tell the story of the Nazis' rise to power and of the major battles of the war. All the films contrasted the threatened free world with the barbaric "Slave World." Capra used exaggerated stereotypes of the enemy countries while idealizing the Allies.

He returned to Hollywood after the war. It was a boom period for the movies, but Frank Capra was no longer the top director. He said he felt a "loneliness that was laced with fear of failure." He was also disillusioned by the side of humanity he had seen during the war. "I thought that perhaps I had put too much faith in the human race . . . in the pictures I made. Maybe they were too much as things should be. I began to think that maybe I was a Pollyanna."

In 1945, with two other producer-directors, he started Liberty Films, an independent production company. Its formation coincided with the end of Hollywood's heyday, however, and Capra was able to make only two films (and no profit) for his company.

Nevertheless, the first of these, *It's a Wonderful Life* (1947), is now considered Capra's masterpiece. It is praised for its technical virtuosity (acting, lighting, the use of flashback, the visual and verbal humor) and for embodying all of Capra's concerns in the perfect film. The British critic Robin Wood called it one of the greatest American films. The story was originally sent as a

George Bailey (James Stewart) stands up to Potter (Lionel Barry-more) in *It's a Wonderful Life*, RKO, 1947. *Museum of Modern Art, Film Stills Archive.*

Christmas card by a writer to his friends. For Capra, "It was the story I had been looking for all my life. Small town. A man. A good man, ambitious. But so busy helping others, life seems to pass him by. Despondent. He wishes he'd never been born. He gets his wish. Through the eyes of a guardian angel he sees the world as it would have been had he not been born." Capra wanted his film to show that "each man's life touches so many other lives."

　　Although many writers worked on the script, Capra wrote the final version himself. He used many actors who had appeared in his other films. James Stewart, who played the lead, George Bailey, said this was his favorite performance.

Capra has called this film his "most personal work." Critics point out that George Bailey's ups and downs are similar to those of Capra, whose downs included the death of a young son in 1935. George is also Capra's most complex character. He is fighting an immoral enemy (Potter, the town's greedy banker, who wants to drive out his Building and Loan). He is also suffering an internal conflict between his own acute desire for success and adventure and his responsibility to his father and to the working people of the town to save the Building and Loan and the many homes it represents.

Capra's second and last Liberty Film was *State of the Union* (1948), the story of an idealistic businessman who compromises his principles while running for office. Even with Katharine Hepburn and Spencer Tracy as its stars, the film did not make enough profit to save Liberty Films. The company was taken over by Paramount. Capra made four more feature films, two of them remakes of his own earlier films. He now had less control than ever before, and these four pictures are inferior to his other films. After suffering severe cluster headaches throughout the production of his last film in 1961 (*A Pocketful of Miracles*), he retired.

Critics have offered several explanations for why, after thirty-six feature films, Capra's career petered out. Some say that in *It's a Wonderful Life* Capra achieved all his artistic goals and had nothing left to strive for. Others blame the experience of World War II. Others claim that he lost his touch, or that a changing world had no place for him. It is true that Capra's optimistic message seemed out of tune with the feelings of Americans during the cold war of the 1950s. Capra himself blames his failure on the abandonment of Liberty Films and the compromising of his one man, one film principle. "It was a thing in my life I've regretted ever since."

He did not stay idle, however. He made some educational science films, worked on his autobiography, and in the 1970s became a popular speaker at film festivals. In 1975 he said, "I feel as useful today as I did at any time in my life."

On April 4, 1982, Frank Capra won the American Film Institute's Life Achievement Award. The citation read: "Frank Capra has ennobled his audience as he has entertained them. His work has brought the meaning of the American dream alive for generations of moviegoers past and present."

# HOWARD HAWKS

ho Is Howard Hawks?" was the title of an article in a film magazine in the 1960s. Hawks had by then not only directed, but produced most of his thirty-nine films, largely on subjects he chose and from scripts he wrote or helped to write. Yet because he had worked in many different popular genres—action films, war films, comedies, gangster films, private eye films, and Westerns—and in a style that didn't call attention to itself, his name was virtually unknown.

Hawks's own artistic claims were always modest. "I try to tell my story as simply as possible," he once said, "with the camera at eye level. I think a director's a storyteller, and if he tells a story that people can't understand, then he shouldn't be a director." Another time he described a director as "somebody who doesn't annoy you." Yet when Hawks was awarded an honorary Oscar in 1975 (his first, though most of his films were box office successes), he was hailed as "a giant of the American cinema whose pictures, taken as a whole, represent one of the most consistent, vivid, and varied bodies of work in world cinema."

Howard Hawks was born on May 30, 1896, in Goshen, Indiana, where his father was a successful paper manufacturer. If his family hadn't moved to California for his mother's health when he was ten, he might never have gone into the movies. As a child he wanted to be an engineer. He was sent east to prep school and then went to Cornell University, where he earned his degree in mechanical engineering. During the summers he worked in the prop department at Famous Players–Lasky, and it was there that he got his first permanent job.

His working methods, however, came from engineering, which "is a process of putting everything on paper or making a visualization of your project. . . . Being trained that way, I never make a scene without first getting a visualization of it. I have artists paint me the scene in complete detail, lighting and shading it as I see it in my mind. . . ." This training also enabled him to design and build a complicated camera car from which to shoot the live-action hunting scenes in *Hatari!* (1962).

Another car he helped to design won the Indianapolis 500 in 1936. Racing cars was a lifetime passion for Hawks and for two or three years a successful career. He had many outdoor passions, which are reflected in the subject matter of his films, including sailing, skiing, riding horses and motorcycles, hunting, fishing, and tennis. He was an excellent gunsmith, silversmith, and carpenter. He was also briefly a professional baseball pitcher and, during World War I, a flying instructor for the Army Air Corps.

By the time he left for the war Hawks had graduated to assistant director for Mary Pickford's films. He
had even shot some scenes on his own when the director
didn't show up one morning. When he returned to Hollywood after the war, he used money he had inherited to
make some one-and two-reel comedies, which he then
sold at a profit to the studios. He did everything on these
films himself, from producing and directing to driving the
cars for the stunts. "I got my training making these . . .,"
he said, "thorough comedy training."

He also took a job at Paramount as a story editor
and producer. He bought stories for more than forty
films, cast them, hired the writers and directors, and
supervised. He went on to head the story department at
MGM, but was tired of writing for other people and quit
when he wasn't given a chance to direct. Hawks educated
himself as a director by watching movies every night for
six months. "And if I thought the movie was worth studying, I saw it twice that same night until I felt I knew
enough to direct. I learned right in the beginning from
Jack Ford, and I learned what not to do by watching
Cecil De Mille."

In 1926, Hawks was hired as a contract director
by the Fox studio, where he wrote and directed his first
film, *The Road to Glory* (1926). This was a tragic story of
a girl going blind. The reaction of the Fox executives was:
"You've shown you can make a picture, but for God's
sake, go out and make entertainment." From then on,
that was Hawks's goal. He soon discovered that he was
naturally in tune with movie audiences, and rarely
needed to preview his films. "I work on the fact that if I
like somebody and think they're attractive, I can make
them attractive. If I think a thing's funny, the people
laugh at it. If I think a thing's dramatic, the audience
does. I'm very lucky that way."

Hawks quit Fox in 1929 to make films independently. He never signed another long-term contract with a studio and quit several films because of studio interference. But because of his success at the box office, he usually had good relations with the studios, which were happy to share in the profits of films he had developed and helped to pay for.

During those early years Hawks did some technical experimenting. In *Paid to Love* (1927), about a prince who falls in love with a Parisian showgirl, he used some of the expressionistic camera tricks brought to Hollywood by the German directors. But he soon gave this up. "Once in a while," he said, "I'll move the camera as if a man were walking and seeing something. And it falls back or it moves in for emphasis when you don't want to make a cut. But, outside of that, I just use the simplest camera in the world."

He tried to simplify the acting style, too. "In those days," he said, "scenes were overplayed. And I started to underwrite." He cut down the dialogue and encouraged a natural, casual style of acting.

Hawks was unemployed for about a year and a half when sound pictures first came in and all the studios were scrambling around for directors with stage experience. He actually considered sound pictures easier to make than silents. "You had to have action when you were making a silent picture. And it had to look good in motion. . . . When dialogue started, it was easy. I can do three times as much work writing dialogue as I can thinking up things to do in action." He also believed that his lack of stage experience contributed to the realism of his films. "Perhaps it is because I have had absolutely no stage training that I don't believe a vehicle should emerge letter-perfect as it was written. If my players are good enough . . . I don't bother directing them at all. I let them interpret their scenes in their own way and ad lib if they like."

Hawks was known for rewriting on the set. "I don't think any action picture is thoroughly worked out. You can't write an action picture: you have to get out and get ready to make it. The form of the picture and the sequence of the picture and everything is worked out. But if the writer puts in the fact that somebody says something coming into a room on a run, you can't do it. . . . You've got to get your action first and then use your dialogue."

*The Dawn Patrol* (1930) was Hawks's first sound picture. It was about a Royal Air Force commander in World War I who had to send his men into battles they couldn't win. It was seen as an anti-war film, but Hawks said, "I've never made a picture to be anti anything or pro anything."

Hawks got his first critical notice for *Scarface* (1932), his own favorite film. Although his Tony Camonte is based on Al Capone, the film is unlike other gangster pictures popular at the time. First, Hawks added an incestuous tone to the relationship between Tony and his sister Cesca that somehow escaped the censors. He also insisted on showing the childishness of his gangsters, based on his own acquaintance with some while preparing for the film. Tony giggles like a six-year-old boy with a new toy as he tries out the portable machine guns he has taken from rival gangsters.

Hawks used lighting deliberately in his films. In many, hanging kerosene lamps provide a warm enclosing glow, and in *El Dorado* (1966) a slash of light coming from the saloon across the street recalls Remington's famous paintings of the West. *Scarface* is darkly shadowed, and in this and other films he often had action scenes take place at night. "You're able to light the set so the audience sees what you want them to see."

Unidentified actor, Paul Muni, Karen Morley, and George Raft in *Scarface*, United Artists, 1932. *Museum of Modern Art, Film Stills Archive.*

This film is also an example of Hawks's ability to combine drama and comedy. "Whenever I hear a story," he said, "my first thought is how to make it into a comedy, and I think of how to make it into a drama only as a last resort." Existing in a world of intense brutality is Tony's comical "seckatary," a man who can't write and who pulls his gun on the telephone when he thinks the caller has insulted him. When a woman tells Tony his apartment is "gaudy," he responds proudly, "Ain't it though?"

Hawks made this film independently with the backing of the aeronautics magnate Howard Hughes. When the studios refused to lend him any stars, he created his own, along with a reputation as a star maker.

Paul Muni (Tony) was playing old men in the Jewish theater in New York when Hawks found him; George Raft (Tony's lieutenant, Guino) he saw at a prize fight carrying a gun; and Ann Dvorak (Cesca) was a chorus girl at MGM. Her tough, sexy character would appear again and again in Hawks's films.

*Scarface* was only slightly marred by the censors, who held it up for a year and a half and then demanded a scene be added in which a newspaper editor talks to a citizens' group about cracking down on organized crime. Hawks refused to shoot this scene himself.

Hawks made two screwball comedies in the 1930s, *Twentieth Century* (1934) and *Bringing Up Baby* (1938). He said he liked to make comedies because "I like to go into a theater and hear people laughing—the more laughter the better I feel."

*Twentieth Century* is based on a play about a stage director (John Barrymore) and the star he creates and tries to control (Carole Lombard). She rebels and sets off on her own, leaving him to a sinking career. In the end, however, he wins her back and is seen ordering her about on the stage, just as at the beginning—a narrative structure Hawks often favored. The comedy depends on the characters and the contrast of real emotions and exaggerated theatrics.

Hawks said he paced his comedies about 20 percent faster than any films before. He took his cue from the two-reelers he had made, which also had given him a taste for visual comedy. "Almost every picture that I make is first funny silent," he said. "It doesn't depend on lines."

He achieved the fast pace not by cutting but by overlapping the dialogue. Before *Twentieth Century*, he said, "actors wouldn't jump on anybody's lines." He added a few unnecessary words at the beginning of each line—"Well," or "I think"—so that the sense would not be lost when the lines overlapped.

*Twentieth Century* established Carole Lombard, an obscure bathing beauty, as a comedienne. Hawks loved her natural, uninhibited craziness but he had to badger it out of her on the set. "Just be yourself," he told her, "and if you don't go and do any goddam thing that you feel like doing, I'm going to fire you and get another girl."

To the play Hawks added a significant detail: the pin which Barrymore uses to poke a realistic scream from Lombard, and which she then preserves as a token of love. He often used symbolic objects to speak for his characters. Throughout *El Dorado*, James Caan wears the funny-looking hat that is all he has left of a friend whose death he is intent to avenge. And in many of his films Hawks has his actors exchange cigarettes to show a close personal relationship.

In addition to being a star-maker, Hawks also was known for using familiar stars in unfamiliar roles. In *Bringing Up Baby*, he gave Cary Grant his first slapstick role, as a stiff, absentminded paleontologist, and Katharine Hepburn her dizziest role, as an heiress who falls in love with him and teaches him that there is more to life than old bones. In the last scene she climbs up the scaffolding to where he has been carefully reconstructing a precariously balanced dinosaur and manages to topple everything over.

Hawks liked to direct stars, what he called "personalities," rather than actors. He could work out scenes for them, knowing what to expect, and would always change the script on the set to fit the words to them rather than the reverse. The overall result in his best films, according to critic Gerald Mast, is that "the stars are the characters and the characters are the stories."

Hawks used Grant in three other comedies and a film about flying. In *His Girl Friday* (1940) Grant costars with Rosalind Russell, who plays a much more aggressive character than ever before. She is Hildy, a newspaper reporter who thinks she wants to leave her career to be a wife and mother. Grant, her former editor and also her former husband, campaigns to win her back for the paper and himself. In the original play, the two main characters were both men, and Hawks's change added a new dimension to the story.

In *I Was a Male War Bride* (1949) Grant is the "alien spouse of female military personnel en route to the United States under Public Law 27." In *Monkey Business* (1952) he is a chemist who invents a rejuvenation drug that gets out of control.

In *Only Angels Have Wings* (1939) he runs an airline, flying the mails over the mountains of a South American country. Two of the film's themes—professionalism and group relationships—are the ones that critics often associate with Hawks. "Professionals are the only people I'm interested in. . . . I'm interested in the guys who are good," he said. And "the best drama for me is the one which shows a man in danger. There is no action where there is no danger."

At the beginning of *Angels*, a pilot who had shown cowardice in the past by abandoning his plane and his copilot is isolated from the rest of the men. By the end, however, he has proven his courage by landing a burning plane and has bandaged hands to show for it. One of the other fliers lights his cigarette for him marking his integration into the group.

This film is often given as an example of Hawks's stoicism. "Who's Joe?" Grant asks when told that one of his pilots had died. "I take a great big situation and play it way down," Hawks said. "The men that I show and choose to show, they don't dramatize these things, they

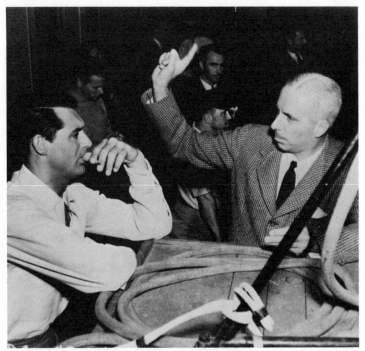

Howard Hawks with Cary Grant on set of *His Girl Friday,* Columbia, 1940. *Museum of Modern Art, Film Stills Archive.*

underplay them." Hawks himself is said to have commented when he heard of the accidental death of a stuntman he had worked with often, "Well, we all get killed sooner or later."

Hawks's comedies have detractors as well as fans, but most critics admire *Only Angles Have Wings.* When it was released, however, it was criticized for not being realistic. Hawks defended it saying, "I knew every character personally that was in that picture. I knew how they talked. And if they began to talk too much because the writer put in too much, I'd just say, 'Cut it out.' . . . There wasn't one scene in the whole picture that wasn't real."

Hawks influenced the careers of two other actors—Lauren Bacall and John Wayne. When Hawks first saw her, Bacall was an eighteen-year-old model with a squeaky voice. He told her he needed an actress with a cool voice, and she screamed her lungs out in the Hollywood Hills until she had it. He also brought out her sex appeal. For *To Have and Have Not* (1944) he told her to be insolent to Humphrey Bogart and had her walk out on him at the end of every scene. (In real life the two were falling in love.) Bacall said of Hawks, "He created me. He was a real movie maker. He loved to work with relationships. He gave actors their head and then used the reality of those situations."

Hawks himself has said, "When I'm making a picture I make it known to the crew that if they've got a suggestion, for goodness sake, make it—and out of it comes some of the best stuff."

*To Have and Have Not* is a very loose adaptation of a Hemingway novel, which Hawks wrote on a hunting and fishing trip with the writer. The most famous line of the film wasn't even in the book: "You don't have to say anything and you don't have to do anything. . . . Oh, maybe just—whistle." He wrote this for Bacall's screen test and Jack Warner, head of the studio, liked it so much he had to find a place for it in the film.

Hawks took the relationship of the two main characters from the book and decided to tell the story of how they met. That relationship is the point of the film, not the plot, in which Bogart grudgingly helps the Free French against the Vichy government in Martinique. "We had to have a plot," Hawks said, " . . . but it was just an excuse for some scenes."

In many of Hawks's films the characters call each other by nicknames. In *To Have and Have Not* Bogart and Bacall call each other Steve and Slim, the nicknames Hawks and his second wife Nancy used for each other.

Hawks married (and divorced) three women, all tall and thin: Athole Shearer, sister of the actress Norma Shearer; Nancy Gross, a model; and Dee Hartford, another model. Hawks himself was a very attractive man, a "mysteriously romantic fashion plate," according to the screenwriter Ben Hecht.

*The Big Sleep* (1946), in which Bogart plays Philip Marlowe, Raymond Chandler's private eye, had an even weaker plot than *To Have and Have Not*. Hawks said that during the making of this picture he discovered "that you don't have to be too logical. You really should just make good scenes. You follow one scene with another and stop worrying about hooking them together." One result is a wonderful seduction scene with Dorothy Mann, proprietor of the bookstore where Marlowe waits for the man he is shadowing. "People remember that scene," Hawks said. "That wasn't the way it was written at all. We just did it because the girl was so damn good looking."

Another result is that many threads of the plot are left untied, including the explanation for one of the murders. But the focus is on relationships, and in an odd twist for this genre, the detective gets the girl. This meant that Hawks had to change the nature of the two main characters and alter the ending of Chandler's novel so that Bacall did not turn out to be the murderer.

John Wayne starred in most of Hawks's Westerns, his favorite genre. Hawks developed the screen character Wayne would play over and over—solid, strong, and inflexible, yet vulnerable. Their first film, *Red River* (1948), is a story of the first cattle drive from Texas to Kansas on the Chisholm Trail. On one level it is an epic, with many characters, a vast geographical area, a long time span, and majestic visual qualities. On another it is the story of a relationship—between Tom Dunson (Wayne) and Matthew Garth (Montgomery Clift). Dunson, who has left a wagon train and a woman to build his own ranch, takes on Garth, an orphaned boy, and raises him almost as a son. When the markets for beef dry up in Texas, Dunson sets out with his herd for Kansas. The route proves too hard, but he refuses to change it. To save the herd and the drive, Garth deposes him. In the end the two are reconciled and Garth's M is added to the Red River D brand.

Hawks slashed huge chunks of dialogue from the script for this film without losing any of the meaning. For instance, he gives Groot, the cook (Walter Brennan), just a few choice words to explain his long, complex relationship with Dunson: "Me and Dunson . . . well, it's me and Dunson."

In the opening of *Rio Bravo* (1959), Hawks eliminates words entirely. He uses actions to establish the situation, the relationships among the characters, and the issues that concern them. A sheriff (Wayne) bursts into a bar to arrest a murderer, and his former crack deputy, now a pathetic drunk, comes to his aid. The film is the story of the sheriff, who with his few men tries to hold the brother of a local gangster in jail until he can be tried for murder. But it really revolves around the deputy (Dean Martin) and his salvation, with Wayne's help.

Hawks has said that most of the movies he made were about "a relationship with two friends." One way of establishing that, he said, is in "little things where one helps the other," gestures revealing the depth of their friendship. He often added this "elaboration of the characters" on the set. "We'd say, 'Now here we have a scene: let's put a little character in it. What do you think this man would do?'" Throughout *Rio Bravo*, for example, Martin kept trying to roll cigarettes unsuccessfully and Wayne would pass one to him. "That grew out of Martin's asking me one day, 'Well, if my fingers are shaking, how can I roll this thing?' So Wayne said,

'Here, I'll help you,' and suddenly we had something going." *Rio Bravo* is generally considered the best and most typical of Hawks's later films. Though it deals with serious situations, it has the humor that *Red River* lacks.

Hawks made five more films, including two more Westerns, the last in 1970, and continued to plan further projects. He also continued to ride motorcycles, tinker with car motors, and make silver jewelry and oak furniture. But in December of 1977, at the age of eighty-one and in relatively good health, he stumbled and fell on the stone floor of his home. He was alone and unconscious for more than twenty-four hours. Though he was able to express his wish to spend his last days at home, he never fully recovered, and he died on December 26, 1977.

By the time the obituaries were being written, moviegoers knew who Howard Hawks was, and Vincent Canby could write of him in the *New York Times*, "Working within the confines of the commercial cinema, Mr. Hawks created a kind of mass entertainment that revealed a true art."

# ALFRED HITCHCOCK

old that moviegoers identified him with the sinister characters and cold suspense of his films, Hitchcock replied, "If they did but realize it, I'm more scared than they are by things in real life." He said that fear, which he passed on to his vast audiences, was "the root of my work" and traced its source to his own childhood.

Alfred Joseph Hitchcock was born in London on August 13, 1899, the third child of a doting mother and a strict father. His father, a successful greengrocer, was a devout Catholic and sent his children to parochial schools. Although critics debate the importance of religion to Hitchcock's work, the films undeniably explore moral dilemmas and guilt, and the human potential for evil.

Perhaps it was the strictness rather than the religion of his childhood that marked Hitchcock. He clearly remembered the hard rubber cane used at school. "I was terrified of physical punishment," he said, and had a "fear of being involved in anything evil." And often he told the story of being sent to the police station when he was about five with a note from his father. The police chief locked him in a cell for several minutes, saying, "This is what we do to naughty boys."

Alfred actually was a solitary, well-behaved child. As a hobby, he collected maps and timetables for ships, subways, and trains, and he liked to watch murder trials at the Old Bailey. His parents whetted his interest in the theater, but he began going to movies on his own, preferring the technically more sophisticated American imports. From the age of sixteen on, he saw as many films as he could and read all the technical and trade magazines. It was about this time also that he discovered the works of Edgar Allan Poe and was drawn to suspense as a literary genre. Hitchcock said he, like Poe, strived to tell "a completely believable story . . . with such spellbinding logic that you get the impression that the same thing could happen to you tomorrow."

His father died when he was fifteen, and Alfred had to go to work. Having spent some time at a school of engineering and navigation, he was able to get a job as a technical clerk at a company that made electrical cables. Soon, however, he discovered an interest in art and began taking drawing courses at night.

In 1920 he learned that an American movie production company was opening a branch for international productions in London, and he applied for a job immediately. Alfred Hitchcock was an odd young man, already unattractively fat. At the age of twenty-one, he had never been out with a girl and still reported the day's events to his mother each evening from the foot of her bed. But he got the job he wanted, writing and designing the title cards for silent films, and tried to learn everything he could from the American actors, writers, and directors. Because the crew was small, he was asked to help finish one film when the director quit, and he was then assigned to direct another until funds ran out.

The company failed, however, after two years, and the studio was rented to British production companies. Hitchcock became an assistant director for the British producer Michael Balcon, and between 1923 and 1925 he designed sets and costumes, wrote scripts, and was an editor and production manager, too.

There he met and worked with the talented film editor Alma Reville. In 1926 she became his wife, adviser, and general critic, giving up her own career and her religion for him. The union was more professional than passionate. (Hitchcock said late in his life that he had been celibate for the last forty years.) But they did have a daughter, Patricia, born in 1928. She studied to be an actress and appeared in small roles in a number of her father's films before her marriage.

In 1925 Balcon asked Hitchcock to direct two productions, to be filmed in Germany. There Hitchcock had the opportunity to watch F. W. Murnau, one of the great innovative directors. His next film, *The Lodger* (1926), showed the influence of what he had seen: the use of light and shadow and strange camera angles to create atmosphere, and the presentation of ideas in visual terms.

Hitchcock called *The Lodger* his "first picture." It is the story of a man who is courting his landlord's daughter. The lodger's mysterious comings and goings raise suspicion that he is guilty of a series of local murders of young blonde women. His real mission, in fact, is to avenge his own sister's killing. In a famous example of visual storytelling, a man's hand is seen sliding down the boardinghouse banister; next comes a pan shot of the eerie stairwell as he goes out into the dark; and then a shot of a newspaper headline reporting another murder.

With *The Lodger*, Hitchcock established a style of working that would change little throughout his career. For the screenplay, he said, "What I do is to read a story only once and if I like the basic idea, I just forget all about the book and start to create cinema." The screenwriter's role was limited by Hitchcock's constant involvement and also his attitude toward dialogue: "We should resort to dialogue only when it's impossible to do otherwise. I always try first to tell a story in the cinematic way, through a succession of shots and bits of film in between." According to the screenwriter for *Vertigo* (1958), for instance, "Hitchcock knew exactly what he wanted to do in this film, exactly what he wanted to say, and how it should be seen and told. I gave him the characters and the dialogue he needed to develop the story, but it was from first frame to last his film."

Hitchcock and his writers always broke down the script into separate shots, which he and an illustrator then drew onto storyboards. The result, he said, was a "precut picture . . . every piece of film is designed to perform a function" (a frustration to producers who liked to cut and paste at the editing stage). Everything from camera angles to set design to props was indicated, and Hitchcock concerned himself with the smallest details. In *Dial M for Murder* (1954), he decided that Grace Kelly's clothes should go from bright to dark, along with her character's fortunes. In *Strangers on a Train* (1951) he selected the debris to surround a cigarette lighter (a vital clue) that falls into a sewer. Hitchcock related his filmmaking techniques to his personal need for order: "I'm full of fears and I do my best to avoid difficulties and any kind of complications. I like everything around me to be clear as crystal and completely calm."

*The Lodger* introduced two themes that would continue to concern Hitchcock: chaos erupting in a comfortable, respectable setting and the innocent man implicated in a crime by circumstantial evidence. French critics and admirers identified another theme, which they called "transfer of guilt." In *The Lodger,* a policeman, who was the original suitor of the landlord's daughter, almost becomes a murderer himself in his zeal to arrest the lodger. In addition, viewers, like the daughter, find themselves being drawn to the man who seems to be a killer.

This film also contains the first of Hitchcock's cameo appearances—in a newspaper office, with his back to the camera. In this film his presence was purely functional, he said. "We had to fill up the screen." Later it became a trademark. His favorite bit part was in *Lifeboat* (1944), a technically challenging film shot entirely in a boat. The shooting coincided with one of Hitchcock's diets (he went from 300 to 200 pounds). In an old newspaper found on the boat, before-and-after photos of him appear in an ad for an imaginary product called Reduco.

*The Lodger* was acclaimed immediately as the greatest British film ever made. Although Hitchcock's next two films for Balcon were not nearly as successful, in 1927 he was offered three times his salary, more freedom, and bigger budgets to join British International Pictures. In five years there he made four silent films and six talkies, most of which do not compare with his later British films and his American films.

His best silent film was *The Ring* (1927)—the "next Hitchcock film" after *The Lodger,* he said. This story of two prizefighters in love with the same woman is notable for its realistic setting and its depiction of lower-class British life. The "ring" is the fighting arena, a wedding band, and also a snakelike bracelet the woman either shows off or hides, depending on her relations with the two men.

Among the other BIP films, *Blackmail* (1929) is important as Britain's first talking picture, though it was conceived and shot as a silent movie. Noises, music, and some dialogue were added later. The film has many trick shots and a striking sound sequence. A woman who stabbed and killed a man who tried to rape her the night before listens to a discussion of the crime over breakfast. The voices overlap, and all she hears is the word "knife" over and over.

*Murder!* (1930) was one of Hitchcock's rare whodunits. These differ from the suspense plots he preferred because "all the interest is concentrated in the ending . . . rather like a jigsaw puzzle or a crossword puzzle. No emotion."

After finishing his commitment to BIP and making a film he hated (*Waltzes from Vienna*, 1933) for an independent producer, Hitchcock was at his lowest ebb professionally. He took a job with Michael Balcon again at Gaumont-British and recouped his fame with *The Man Who Knew Too Much* (1934). In this picture a family of British tourists in Switzerland witness the assassination of a Frenchman. Before he dies he tells them of a plot by an anarchist group to murder a foreign diplomat in London. To silence the tourists, the anarchists kidnap their daughter. The film is about their attempt to get her back and stop the murder.

The anarchists' goal was what Hitchcock called a "McGuffin" and used often—the excuse for the plot, something of great importance to the characters which never has to be explained logically. His favorite McGuffin was the unexplained "government secrets" being sought by spies in *North by Northwest* (1959), because it was the "simplest, most non-existent, and the most absurd."

The two outstanding films among his six for Balcon were *The Lady Vanishes* (1938) and *The Thirty-Nine Steps* (1935), one of Hitchcock's favorites. *The Lady Vanishes*, with its characteristic Hitchcock blend of tension and comedy, is about a young woman who starts a conversation with an old governess on a train. When the governess, Mrs. Froy (Dame May Whitty), mysteriously disappears, the other passengers, members of a spy ring, deny her existence and suggest the woman was hallucinating. Hitchcock was able to use the models and technical effects he loved for this film. All the train cars but one were either transparencies or miniatures.

In *The Thirty-Nine Steps*, a murder is committed in the rented room of a young man, who flees the police to search for those responsible. This movie is full of action and quick escapes. "I saw it as a film of episodes," Hitchcock said. "I made sure the content of every scene was very solid, so that each one would be a little film in itself." Hitchcock also used his first cold but sensuous blonde, Madeleine Carroll, who reluctantly accompanies the hero (she's handcuffed to him). "Sex on the screen," he said, "should be suspenseful."

Another film from this period introduces what came to be a Hitchcock characteristic. The villain in *The Secret Agent* (1936), Robert Young, is very attractive and sympathetic. Because he is so appealing to the audience, his deeds are that much more repellent.

In 1937 Hitchcock took a transatlantic trip to meet with American studio heads. Two years later he accepted an exclusive seven-year contract with David O. Selznick at United Artists, although he was lent out to other studios for all but three films. In Hollywood, Hitchcock continued to live his private, essentially British life, not becoming an American citizen until 1955. He ignored the Beverly Hills party circuit, but continued to court the press, as he had always done in England.

Most critics don't like Hitchcock's early American films as well as some of the later ones. He himself complained of casting problems. Because the thriller was looked down on when he first came to America, he often couldn't attract the actors he wanted and was sometimes forced to use inappropriate ones who happened to be under contract to the studios. The smooth Louis Jourdan, for instance, played what should have been a coarse character in *The Paradine Case* (1948).

*Rebecca* (1940), his first American film, was a commercial success but not, he said, "a Hitchcock film." Selznick, a stubborn and very involved producer, insisted that the film be faithful to the Daphne du Maurier novel. As a result, Hitchcock said, "The story is lacking in humor." His philosophy, he said, was that "after a certain amount of suspense the audience must find relief in laughter."

Joan Fontaine, who played the female lead in *Rebecca*, was the first to complain about Hitchcock's treatment of actresses: "He wanted total control over me." Anne Baxter, who starred in *I Confess* (1953), had a similar complaint: "There was a lot of Pygmalion in him, and he was proud of how he transformed actresses." This tendency seems to have reached a peak with Tippi Hedren (*The Birds*, 1963; *Marnie*, 1964). He tried to dictate whom she saw and what she wore even off the set. When she turned down a sexual proposition while shooting *The Birds*, she said he threatened to ruin her career and acted vindictively toward her during the rest of the filming. For one terrifying scene he decided to use live birds to attack her rather than the safer mechanical ones.

Hitchcock's biographers have accounted for this behavior in two ways. First, Hitchcock thought actors were secondary to the visual aspect of a film, and he often left the casting until late in the preparatory period. Actors, he said, "should be willing to be utilized and wholly integrated into the picture by the director and the camera." He was not interested in psychological direction or method acting and did not allow improvisation on

Alfred Hitchcock coaching his daughter Patricia for her small role in *Strangers on a Train*, Warner Brothers, 1951. *Museum of Modern Art, Film Stills Archive.*

the set. Secondly, according to Donald Spoto, Hitchcock's most recent and probing biographer, he also had an ambivalent attitude toward women, based on a fear of being unable to control his own erotic longings.

One of Hitchcock's favorite American films was *Shadow of a Doubt* (1943). "It was the blending of character and thriller at the same time," he said. "That's very hard to do." Uncle Charlie (Joseph Cotton) visits his family in a small American town. His adoring niece (named Charlie also and his counterpart in a number of ways) gradually discovers he is a murderer of wealthy widows. When her uncle tries to silence her, he dies himself, under the wheels of a train. This film illustrates Hitchcock's concern with the details of location. He chose a real town for the setting and a real house for the exterior shots, hired some local people as actors, and held Uncle Charlie's funeral in the town square.

During World War II, Hitchcock went back to England for a short stint. He made two propaganda films and visited his mother and brother, who were both sick and who died before the war was over. When he returned to America, he discovered to his delight that one of Selznick's biggest new stars, Ingrid Bergman, was a perfect Hitchcock blonde. Her first film for him, *Spellbound* (1945), was marred by its simplistic psychoanalytic theme. But the next, *Notorious* (1946), is, according to filmmaker and critic François Truffaut, "the very quintessence of Hitchcock." Alicia (Bergman), the playgirl daughter of a convicted traitor, is sent by the Secret Service to infiltrate a group of her father's Nazi friends in South America. She marries one of them, a sweetly compelling villain played by Claude Rains, but he soon finds her out and begins to poison her. Cary Grant, the U.S. agent in charge, finally comes to her rescue. Underlying the suspense plot is a story of passionate love between Grant and Bergman, threatened by mistrust and misunderstanding.

This film contains a famous example of Hitchcock's visual storytelling. A track shot begins at the top of a stairway, goes through a crowded room, and finally focuses on a key in Alicia's hand. According to Hitchcock, the camera was saying, "There's a large reception being held in this house, but there is a drama here which no one is aware of, and at the core of that drama is this tiny object."

Donald Spoto called *Notorious* "one of [Hitchcock's] most alarmingly personal films—full of repressed passion, desire and danger, and the conflicts of duty." He also points out that, like Hitchcock, Rains reports to his mother from the foot of her bed.

After his contract with Selznick ended in the late 1940s, Hitchcock made deals with an independent company and then with Warner Brothers, Paramount, and Universal. By now, he was in almost complete control of the choice of subjects, writers, and casts for his films. Yet he began drinking heavily and eating voraciously, and his first films during this period seem most interesting for technical reasons.

In *Rope* (1948), for instance—about a murder committed by the hosts before a dinner party and discovered by one of the guests at the end—Hitchcock filmed the complete story with no editing. He shot in ten-minute takes (the length of a roll of film) and disguised the breaks. "The motion of the camera and the movement of the players," he said, "closely followed my usual cutting practice. In other words, I maintained the rule of varying the size of the image in relation to its emotional importance within a given episode."

Hitchcock's most creative period began with *Strangers on a Train* (1951), a clear example of two of his

Alicia (Ingrid Bergman) with key in her hand, *Notorious*, RKO, 1946.
*Museum of Modern Art, Film Stills Archive.*

favorite themes: transfer of guilt and the idea that destructive impulses exist in all of us and must be actively restrained. On a train, Bruno, a mad, rich, young dissolute who hates his father, meets Guy, a tennis champion who is trying to get a divorce in order to remarry. Bruno proposes swapping murders. He will kill Guy's wife and Guy will kill Bruno's father. Thus, no motive will be found for either crime. He then proceeds to do his part. When Guy, who in truth is glad to be free, insists that there was no bargain, Bruno threatens to frame him. In the climactic sequence, Guy races to finish an important match before Bruno can plant his cigarette lighter at the scene of the crime, while the audience finds itself rooting for both men.

Hitchcock's next few films were partly influenced by the screenwriter John Michael Hayes, who stimulated his taste for humor. The dialogue in *Rear Window* (1954), *To Catch a Thief* (1955), *The Trouble with Harry* (1956), and the 1956 remake of *The Man Who Knew Too Much* is lively and sophisticated.

Many critics have called *Rear Window* a classic, and Hitchcock considered it his "most cinematic" film. The opening scene is a perfect example: the camera describes the situation without words by moving from James Stewart's face to his leg cast to a broken camera to magazines to a photograph of a racing car crash. As the film progresses, the news photographer (Stewart), confined to his apartment, peers into the windows of his neighbors across a rear courtyard. He speculates about their lives and begins to suspect one of murder.

In the next series of Hitchcock films, the tone changes. *Vertigo* (1958) is a romantic, obsessive tragedy. A retired policeman with a fear of heights (James Stewart) is asked by a friend from the past to follow his wife Madeleine (Kim Novak), who has been acting suicidal. Stewart falls in love with her, but because of his own vertigo is unable to prevent her from jumping from an old mission tower. Later he thinks he has rediscovered her in another woman, only to lose her again. Stewart attempts to model the second woman in the image of the first, just as Hitchcock often sought to fit his leading ladies into the image of his ideal blonde (Madeleine was a brunette in the book).

Asked about the moral implications of his most famous film, *Psycho* (1960), Hitchcock said, "There's a devil in every one of us." *Psycho* starts out as the story of a secretary (Janet Leigh) who steals $40,000 to start a new life with her lover. She spends the night at a run-down motel operated by a sensitive, attractive young man, Norman Bates (Anthony Perkins). She is killed in a ghastly shower stabbing, apparently by Norman's jealous, possessive mother, whom her son seems to be protecting. Several times in this film Hitchcock gets the audience to identify with the criminal—when Janet Leigh escapes with the money, when Norman is trying to clean her blood from the bathroom, and when he waits for her car to sink into the swamp.

*The Birds* (1963), Hitchcock's most expensive and technically ambitious film, is about "complacency," he said. It is an extreme example of chaos breaking out in the most ordinary setting—an inexplicable and violent attack by birds on a small town near San Francisco. Critics liked the special effects (four hundred trick or composite shots made up about a quarter of the film), but found the characters unmoving.

After several films that were not well received, Hitchcock went to England to film *Frenzy* (1972) with well-known English stage actors. The film was a critical and commercial success. It has the standard Hitchcock theme of a man wrongly accused of having murdered his ex-wife, with the addition of the most violent and repulsive rape-murder scene in any of his films. For comic relief, Hitchcock interjects a dinner scene in which the police inspector's wife serves him a series of unappetizing dishes she has learned to prepare in a gourmet cooking class.

In 1976 Hitchcock finished his fifty-third and last film, *Family Plot*, which got good reviews as a lightweight comic thriller. By now he was drinking more heavily and suffering from an accumulation of health problems, and Alma was seriously disabled from a stroke. He shut his office in May 1979 and the couple became housebound, seeing almost no one except their daughter. Hitchcock died about a year later, on April 29, 1980, leaving an estate of $20 million. This fortune represented not only his astute management of the profits from his movies, but also money from the two weekly television series he supervised and the mystery magazines to which he lent his name.

Although Alfred Hitchcock ultimately won numerous awards and honors—from the Academy of Motion Picture Arts and Sciences, the Screen Producers Guild, the French Order of Arts and Letters, the American Film Institute, and the British government—there is no consensus among critics on his standing as a film artist. Some consider him just a technician and manipulator. But to François Truffaut, one of the French critics who "discovered" Hitchcock in the 1950s, he was "the most complete filmmaker of all."

# GEORGE CUKOR

eorge Cukor kept his personal and professional secrets to himself. He directed feature films, including some of the best and best-loved films of the 1930s, 1940s, and early 1950s. Yet he told critics that a film is a "series of collaborations," and that the chief collaborators are the actors and the writer, not the director. He was "best pleased," he said, "when the finished picture shows the laymen in the audience no visible sign of 'direction,' but mainly seems to be a smooth and convincing presentation by the players of the subject in hand."

Cukor impressed most interviewers with his kindness and his wit, but he never told them very much about his private life. This may have been because he was a homosexual. It was well known in Hollywood and didn't seem to affect his career, but he may have feared that mass audiences would not be so open-minded.

What he did talk about was a youth filled with passion for the theater. George Cukor was born in New York City on July 7, 1899. His parents were well-off Hungarian Jews. His father worked in the district attorney's office and wanted his son to become a lawyer. George, however, was happiest when peering down from the balconies of Broadway theaters. He would go to shows two or three times a week, sometimes playing hooky from school. Although his parents were avid theatergoers themselves, they were not at all pleased when he announced firmly at the age of twelve that he intended to be a director.

In 1918, after a brief stint in the army during World War I, Cukor began a career in the theater that lasted for eleven years. He started out as a stage manager. During the summers he worked for a stock company, where he began to direct. In 1925 he directed his first Broadway play.

When sound was added to the movies about 1929, Hollywood studios hunted desperately for people with stage experience to teach their silent actors how to speak. By then, Cukor had directed many of America's greatest stage actors. He also had earned a reputation for being able to get good performances from talented but temperamental women.

Paramount Studios offered him a job as a dialogue director, and Cukor decided to accept. To his surprise, he liked filmmaking and never regretted his move to Hollywood. As a dialogue director on three films, he shot screen tests and worked with the actors on their intimate scenes. He also taught himself moviemaking techniques by watching more experienced directors at work. Cukor was then asked to co-direct three adaptations of stage plays.

One of these, *The Royal Family of Broadway* (1930), based on the Barrymore family, was "the beginning of a breakthrough for me, making the camera much more mobile." His camera follows Fredric March (the John Barrymore character) up the stairs and through several rooms, discarding his clothes on the way to the bath. Cukor's general "rule of thumb," however, was to be: "Unless moving the camera is going to contribute something to the scene in question, let it remain at rest." What is important, he believed, is to hear the lines. "If you complicate the action or camera work, then the audience has to strain to hear every word."

The first film Cukor directed alone was *Tarnished Lady* (1931), Tallulah Bankhead's first talkie. But studio executives, afraid that the film's satire of high society would offend some prominent people, cut and reshot several scenes. This would not be the last time that interfering producers damaged a Cukor film. *A Life of Her Own* (1950), *The Chapman Report* (1962), and *Justine* (1969) were probably the worst hit, but *A Star Is Born* (1954), with Judy Garland, suffered, too. From a restored version released in 1984, it is clear that important dramatic scenes were sacrificed to make room for an unnecessary musical number.

Yet Cukor always staunchly defended the major studio executives he worked for: "They provided you with the best stories, the best actors, the best technicians, the best scripts. . . . Also there were intelligent restraints: People were not allowed to indulge themselves. . . . if you had anything at all to give they encouraged you. . . . Because it was to their advantage."

In 1932, after two more films for Paramount, Cukor left for RKO, where the producer David Selznick promised him more creative freedom. Five films later he followed Selznick to MGM, where he stayed under contract until the 1950s, when the studio system began to disintegrate. At MGM Cukor had access to Hollywood's best production departments and story properties.

As his films became popular, he also earned some clout. By the mid-1930s Cukor could choose subjects that interested him—often those dealing with social mores. No actor was ever imposed on him. The studio, for instance, wanted the child star Jackie Cooper, to play David Copperfield in his 1935 film. Cukor insisted on an English actor and got him.

*A Bill of Divorcement* (1932) was Cukor's first commercial success and the beginning of a long personal and professional relationship with Katharine Hepburn. They made eight movies and two television films together, including his favorite, *Little Women* (1933), in which she played the spunky sister Jo. For about ten years, beginning in the late 1960s, Hepburn lived in a small guest house in the garden of Cukor's grand estate.

In *A Bill of Divorcement* Hepburn plays a headstrong young woman. Although she had never acted in a film before, Cukor insisted on her for the part. In her screen test, he said, "she placed a glass on the floor and something about that gesture was very, very moving. She was like no one I had ever seen." Of her performance in the film he said, "She had no self-consciousness at all, she was born for the movies although she didn't know it." Katharine Hepburn, like many actors Cukor worked with, came to her first artistic awareness under his direction.

Three male actors won Academy Awards for their performances in George Cukor's films—James Stewart *(The Philadelphia Story)*, Ronald Coleman *(A Double Life)*, and Rex Harrison *(My Fair Lady)*. Yet Cukor is often identified as a woman's director because he directed Hollywood's most talented and high-strung female stars of the 1930s and 1940s to some of their best performances. He got stars like Joan Crawford to put aside their public images for the sake of their roles.

The key to Cukor's success was his respect for

actors and his ability to find the right way to work with each one. He spoke of "the acting gift," and said, "There are some wonderful directors who are much more intrigued by the picture as a whole. They build up an effect of a doorknob turning rather than concentrating on the actor's face. I think human values are more important." As a director he tried to influence performances. "I stimulate their imagination. I give them courage. . . . They know I'm there so if they do make fools of themselves I will most likely pull them together."

Katharine Hepburn said that what distinguishes Cukor's films is that "all the people in his pictures are as good as they can possibly be." Directing her, he had to restrain her tendency to be what he called an "artistic bully." "She's an extremely intelligent woman full of horse sense, and she requires full explanations of every little thing she is doing before the camera."

Greta Garbo, an extremely sensitive actress, starred in Cukor's *Camille* (1937), the story of a young man in love with a beautiful courtesan who is dying of consumption. With Garbo, he said, "You have to give her her head—let her do what she feels." In rehearsal he asked her to play each scene first as she understood it before he offered any suggestions. Yet he recognized his own memory of his mother's recent death "in certain wonderful things she did, the way she used her voice, it was faded and gone."

*The Women* (1939) may have been the greatest challenge to Cukor's ability to handle stars. It is a comedy about infidelity in New York society. There were more than 125 actors, many of them stars and all of them female. For Joan Fontaine the film was a turning point. Fontaine credits Cukor with finally making her into an actress after four years in the movies. "I learned more about acting from one sentence of George Cukor's than from all my years of acting lessons," she said. "Think and

Mary Boland, Rosalind Russell, and Joan Crawford in *The Women*, MGM, 1939. *Museum of Modern Art, Film Stills Archive.*

feel, and the rest will take care of itself." Rosalind Russell successfully played her first comic role as a nasty gossip.

Joan Crawford, who played "the other woman" in *The Women*, appeared in two more Cukor films. According to some critics, *A Woman's Face* (1941) was the best performance of her career. She plays a criminal with a terrible facial scar who reforms after it is removed. Cukor was worried that Crawford would overact. For the courtroom scene where she tells her dramatic life story, "he rehearsed the very life out of me," she said. "Hours of drilling, with camera and lights. . . . *then* Mr. Cukor had me recite the multiplication table by twenties until all emotion was drained and I was totally exhausted, my voice dwindled to a tired monotone."

This film led into a period of straight drama for Cukor, which lasted for most of the 1940s. For one of these films, *Gaslight* (1944), Ingrid Bergman won an Academy Award. She plays the wife of a greedy, evil man who tries to drive her mad so that he can search freely for jewels hidden in her house. In order to maintain Bergman's intensity between takes, Cukor said, "I'd re-tell her the story, the emotional point the scene was leading up to." George Cukor called himself an "interpretive director." Thirty-four of his forty-eight films are adaptations of novels or plays, which he approached with deep respect for the original. "Find out what makes the thing survive, and do that," he said. "Keep the vigor, keep the point of it, but don't try to improve it out of all shape." He acknowledged plot flaws in the novel *Little Women*, for instance, that he did not fix in the film: the invalid sister Beth seems to die several times and the hero doesn't even appear until the last quarter. "It wouldn't have been difficult to reconstruct it, but the trick is always to make a movie of something without rending it apart."

Cukor described his role in developing the scripts for his films as more critic than collaborator. "I'm not a writer, but I know how to tickle screenwriters and make suggestions that will help them improve what they have written." He attended story conferences, contributing ideas about plot and dialogue.

During shooting he followed the finished script strictly, going back to the writer for even small changes in wording. Yet an example he gave from *Justine*, based on Lawrence Durrell's *Alexandria Quartet*, shows how much still was left for the director to do. In one scene, according to the script, Melissa comes out with three other dancers. She is supposed to be inept. "An inept dancer would be pathetic or comic," Cukor said. "The story point is that she doesn't have her heart in it . . . it's all a routine she's bored with. You have to render all that with the business you create for the girl."

Cukor did not approve of improvisation. Improvised dialogue, he said, "has no well-defined tempo; it is slipshod and invariably makes the scene seem listless. . . . The real trick is to make the scene as if it was improvised by giving the performance a sense of spontaneity." There are such scenes in all of his films. He rehearsed his actors without dulling their performances by emphasizing the mechanical elements of scenes instead of their emotions.

The films with which George Cukor is most often associated and which brought him great commercial success are his sophisticated comedies, several starring Katharine Hepburn. *Holiday* (1938), based on a play in which she had been the understudy for the female lead, is about Johnny Case (Cary Grant), a young man who is about to marry into the wealthy Seton family. His fiancée Julia expects him to join her father's bank, but he has idealistic notions about finding himself. These strike a chord in Julia's unconventional sister Linda (Hepburn), who goes off with Johnny in the end.

Cukor said of making plays into films: "You have to move it sometimes very subtly." In *Holiday*, Linda, her brother Ned, Johnny, and two of his friends celebrate New Year's Eve together in the Setons' childhood playroom upstairs, while a stuffy formal party goes on below. Cukor adds action to this confined scene by moving his camera around the room from character to character.

The subtlety with which the romance develops in this film is characteristic of Cukor. In almost all of his films he managed to convey sexual tension without explicit sex. In *The Chapman Report* (1962), about four women who are interviewed for a sex study, he chose a refined actress, Claire Bloom, to play the nymphomaniac in order to give the role an overtone of sadness.

In *The Philadelphia Story* (1940), another romantic comedy, Katharine Hepburn plays the upper-class Tracy Lord. Cary Grant is her prankish former husband, who manages to break through her tough outer crust while disrupting preparations for her second marriage. Since Hepburn had already played her role more than four hundred times on stage, Cukor had to face the possible problem of staleness. "Very often, when they've done it a certain way on the stage, you change it a tiny bit," he said. In this case, he "discombobulated" Hepburn by telling her not to cry at a point when she had cried in the play.

In *Adam's Rib* (1949), Katharine Hepburn and Spencer Tracy play married lawyers who find themselves on opposite sides of a case, which spills over into their private life. Hepburn is defending a woman (Judy Holliday) who shot at her philandering husband, and Tracy is the district attorney.

As always, Cukor thoroughly researched his subject, a process he particularly enjoyed. Before filming, he and Hepburn visited New York City courts to observe the behavior of judges and juries. They watched the trial of a woman who had stabbed and killed someone. "We took pictures of the woman from the time she was first brought in. She looked very tough and made-up before the case started, then she appeared in court very discreetly dressed and quiet and modest (we used this idea for the Judy Holliday character)."

Cukor used long takes in this film to build intensity. In the most striking one, lasting more than seven minutes, Holliday, being interviewed in prison, is seen over Hepburn's shoulder. This is a camera technique Cukor favored. He used long takes noticeably in *A Star Is Born* with Judy Garland and in *A Double Life* (1947) with Ronald Coleman. In that film an actor (Coleman) becomes so involved in playing the role of Othello that he really stabs himself. Before that, in a long take rising in emotion, he tells his life story.

"A scene has to be well written and well played to sustain the audience's interest throughout a long take," Cukor said, "so I only use long takes when I'm sure both the screenplay and the actors are up to it." The screenplays for both *Adam's Rib* and *A Double Life* were written by Ruth Gordon and Garson Kanin, the husband and wife team with whom Cukor worked closely and with great success between 1947 and 1953. They gave him sophisticated, well-written scripts about ordinary people, often women confronting social barriers. Many of the films were set in New York and shot at least partly on location. Judy Holliday for example, travels through New York subways and streets to track down her husband in *Adam's Rib*.

Cukor made several other films with Judy Holliday, whom he considered a "virtuoso" performer. She was able to deliver his kind of comedy, the kind that would "catch you in the throat when you least expect it." She won an Oscar for her portrayal in *Born Yesterday* (1950) of Billie Dawn, a racketeer's dumb blonde ladyfriend who is encouraged to read and think and assert herself. Cukor's film was based on a play by Garson Kanin in which Holliday had starred for four years. Cukor had to rehearse very carefully so that the two male leads were as sure of their roles as she was. He also had to change the staging. While the play takes place in one room, Cukor moves around every room of a huge Washington hotel suite and also shows scenes at the Washington Monument and the Library of Congress.

In *It Should Happen to You* (1954), Holliday plays Gladys Glover, a young woman who wants to become famous. She does—by renting billboards and plastering her name all over New York City. Jack Lemmon plays her

George Cukor (right) with Judy Holliday and William Holden, *Born Yesterday*, Columbia, 1950. *Museum of Modern Art, Film Stills Archive.*

boyfriend. This was his first film with Cukor, and he said he learned his "craft as an actor from Cukor's simple advice: 'Less is more.'" Cukor encouraged actors to bring something of themselves to their roles to make them believable. When a fight scene between Lemmon and Holliday fell flat, Cukor asked him to enact what really happened when he got angry. In the film Lemmon clutches a cramped stomach.

Cukor made two more notable films in the 1950s. *A Star Is Born* (1954) has been praised for the quality of the acting. Judy Garland, who was making a comeback and trying to move away from the cheery musicals she had done before, plays a small-time band singer who is discovered by a famous actor (James Mason), now an alcoholic. The actor's own star finally falls as hers quickly rises. The drunk scenes in this film and many others by Cukor are noticeably sympathetic and nonjudgmental.

*A Star Is Born* was a challenging film for Cukor: it was his first musical, his first color film, and his first film using CinemaScope (wide screen). He met all three challenges successfully. Even in the unrestored version, his careful blend of plot and score is apparent. Unlike conservative directors, who lined up their actors in the middle of the wide screen, Cukor moved his from side to side and sometimes partly off the screen. At one point he places Mason and Garland at opposite sides to show the emotional distance between them. Cukor used both color and light to give his films a natural look. "The film itself has so much color in it," he said, "that the trick is to remove color, to use it only when you really need it, and very sparingly elsewhere."

In *Bhowani Junction* (1956), his only epic, he further developed his skills with color and wide screen. The film takes place as the British are retreating from India. It is concerned with an Anglo-Indian nurse (Ava Gardner) who straddles both worlds. Cukor gave the film a burnt brown color, the way the country looked to him. He made the wide screen seem to shrink and expand, depending on the intimacy of the scenes.

Cukor's next important film was *My Fair Lady* (1964). It was his biggest box office hit and finally won an Academy Award for him, as well as seven other Oscars, including Best Picture. The film was based on the successful Broadway show about a professor of linguistics who trains a flower girl to speak like a princess and then falls in love with her. "What I liked about it," said Cukor, "was the fact that it was less of a romantic love story than a battle of wits."

The film posed familiar problems for Cukor. He tried to add movement to the musical numbers rather than to the dialogue. On the stage, for instance, after Eliza, the transformed flower girl, sang "I Could Have Danced All Night," she fell asleep on the couch. In the film she sings while she dances up the stairs to her bedroom. He also had to tone down the performance of Rex Harrison, who had played Professor Higgins more than a thousand times on the stage. To keep it fresh, Cukor didn't let him rehearse and made him perform his songs live rather than move his lips to prerecordings.

Cukor researched the film in England, walking through blocks of turn-of-the-century houses. "Little details," he said, ". . . bring places and habits to life, like the stuffed animals on the second floor of Professor Higgins's house and the *art nouveau* in his mother's house." The inspiration for the scene in which Eliza's father and a group of workmen sing "With a Little Bit of Luck" came from a painting of the period.

Perhaps because of the strain of making *My Fair Lady* or because of the increasing difficulty of putting together the financial package needed for a movie, Cukor did not work again until he was asked to take over *Justine* from another director in 1969. He was to make

three more films, including *Travels with My Aunt* (1972),
based on the Graham Greene novel, one of his most
visually beautiful films, and *The Blue Bird* (1976), a
disastrous Russian co-production of an allegory by
Maurice Maeterlinck. He also made two television films
starring Katharine Hepburn, one of which won an Emmy
for best direction.

In 1980, at the age of eighty-one, Cukor was asked
to step in as director of *Rich and Famous*, probably
making him the oldest person every to direct a feature
film. This film, his last, was a natural for him. It stars
two movie queens, Candice Bergen and Jacqueline
Bisset, and has a witty script inspired by a play. The film
is about the loving but competitive friendship between
two women from the time they are roommates in college
until they are middle-aged. Cukor treated this serious
subject lightly but with respect and brought out excellent performances from his stars.

George Cukor died of heart failure on January 24,
1983. He had been given a gala retrospective by the Film
Society of Lincoln Center and had won the D. W. Griffith
Award from the Directors Guild of America and the
Golden Lion in Venice for his life work. Yet he has often
been praised faintly for his "taste." He himself summed
up his career modestly in 1971: "I did what I set out to
do—I made them laugh and I made them cry." Perhaps
the critic Andrew Sarris best put Cukor's achievement
into perspective. When a director has consistently provided "tasteful entertainment of a high order," he wrote,
for as long as George Cukor did, he is no "mere enter-
tainer" but "a genuine artist."

# ORSON WELLES

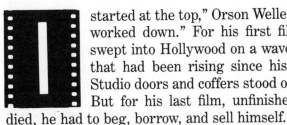

"I started at the top," Orson Welles said, "and worked down." For his first film, he was swept into Hollywood on a wave of success that had been rising since his childhood. Studio doors and coffers stood open to him. But for his last film, unfinished when he died, he had to beg, borrow, and sell himself.

George Orson Welles was born on May 6, 1915, in Kenosha, Wisconsin. His parents were wealthy and prominent. His father was a factory and hotel owner, inventor, and playboy. His mother was a well-known pianist. They treated their precocious son as an adult, and from a very young age he mixed with the artists and intellectuals in their set.

But the Welleses got divorced when Orson was six, and both died during his boyhood—his mother when he was nine and his father when he was fifteen. A family friend, Dr. Maurice Bernstein (whom he memorialized as Kane's faithful general manager in *Citizen Kane*), took over his care and became his official guardian.

Growing up, Welles was widely known as a "boy wonder." He could read fluently at two and by seven knew *King Lear* by heart. Shakespeare became his life-long obsession, and as a child he often staged the plays. He also wrote plays of his own, painted, did magic, and played the violin and piano, which he gave up when his mother died.

His formal education began at the age of ten, when he was sent to a boarding school. There he found another mentor, who encouraged him to follow his interests. In five school years he produced thirty plays. Then, hoping to encourage the boy's artistic talent, Dr. Bernstein sent him on a sketching tour of Europe. But Welles had different plans. In Ireland he bluffed his way onto the stage. At sixteen, smoking a cigar to appear older, he introduced himself at a famous Dublin theater as a Broadway star and was given leading roles there for the next two years.

But even with real reviews attesting to his talent, he couldn't get a job on Broadway. He went home instead, where he annotated and illustrated an edition of Shakespeare for actors. Then he left again to travel in North Africa, and to fight bulls as "The American."

This time when he returned, he had an introduction to Katharine Cornell, one of America's leading stage actresses. She hired him to tour with her company. After a year of that, he began a lucrative radio career. His resonant voice could be heard regularly delivering the news on "The March of Time" and as "The Shadow," a rich playboy who tracked down criminals. He also wrote, directed, starred in, and narrated a weekly program of literary adapations.

During the Depression, Welles was asked to work for the Federal Theater Project, which was intended to create jobs for theater people. He directed an all-black *Macbeth*, set in Haiti, and a famous version of *Dr. Faustus*, performed against a black curtain with no scenery. Funds for these productions were sparse and Welles occasionally gave up his salary or contributed money of his own.

In 1937, after the government tried to stop his production of *The Cradle Will Rock*, an operetta that satirized American politics, Welles and John Houseman formed a repertory company of their own. The Mercury Theater (Welles took the name from a magazine cover) was to perform both classical and modern plays. Eventually it had a theater on Broadway and thirty-four actors. Some of them, including Joseph Cotten, Agnes Moorehead, and Everett Sloane, later went with Welles to Hollywood. After several successful plays, Welles staged a costly failure, *Five Kings*, a two-day performance (fourteen hours) based on Shakespeare's history plays.

Nevertheless, *Time* magazine called him the "brightest moon that has risen over Broadway in years." In 1938 the radio brought him more notoriety. To liven up an adaptation of *The War of the Worlds* by H. G. Wells, he presented it as a news broadcast. Listeners tuning in late heard that Martians were landing all over the United States and killing people with death rays. The people panicked, clogging phone lines and highways.

The name Orson Welles was well known by 1939 when he signed an unprecedented contract with RKO. He was to make a minimum of one film a year, which he could write, direct, produce, and act in. He got an advance of $150,000 plus 25 percent of the gross profits and a guarantee of no interference from the studio. Many

Hollywood regulars hoped to see this brash young man "get his come-uppance," much as the townspeople looked forward to George's come-uppance in *The Magnificent Ambersons* (1942), Welles's second motion picture.

When he first arrived at RKO, Welles was quoted as saying, "This is the biggest electric train set any boy ever had!" He quickly set out to master it. He spent weeks learning about lighting and microphones and screened for himself a library of great American films. His only previous film experience was a four-minute satire he once made of avant-garde films and two short films he used as parts of his plays.

After a few false starts, Welles began work on *Citizen Kane* (1941), which has been compared in its influence to Griffith's *The Birth of a Nation*. The film is essentially a character study of the fictitious Charles Foster Kane (played by Welles). Kane is a powerful press baron whose life, like that of many of Welles's heroes, ends in tragedy. Welles opens the film, as he often does, at the end of the story, with a newsreel of Kane's death. A reporter is assigned to interview the important people in his life to uncover the real Kane and the meaning of his dying word: "Rosebud."

The story is told through flashbacks, which are generally chronological but overlap and conflict because of the different points of view. The opera debut of Kane's second wife Susan, whom he has pushed far beyond her meager talents, is seen through the boredom of his drama critic friend, Susan's own fright, and finally, in a spectacular boom shot, through the disdain of two technicians watching the stage from a scaffold high in the rafters.

There have been two controversies connected with this film. One is based on the striking similarity between Kane and press baron William Randolph Hearst. Welles denied it, but Hearst was convinced that he was being

Editor Kane (Orson Welles, center) with his drama critic (Joseph Cotten) and general manager (Everett Sloane) in *Citizen Kane*, RKO, 1941. *Museum of Modern Art, Film Stills Archive.*

slandered and tried to stop distribution of the film. Some critics also claim that Welles stole credit from his co-writer for the screenplay, which won the film's only Academy Award. It seems unlikely, however, that the material could have been turned into a great film without its director.

*Citizen Kane* has been praised for various techniques that Welles used dramatically. Other directors had put ceilings on their sets, for instance, but Welles used them deliberately to make the indoor scenes more realistic.

Most distinctive was his use of deep focus, which keeps in focus everything from 2 feet to 70 yards from the camera. In a single deep-focus shot, Welles tells the story of Susan's eventual suicide. In the foreground is the poison bottle and a glass, then Susan lying in bed. Farther back is the door to her room, with light coming from under it. On the sound track are her gasps and loud pounding on the door.

Welles achieved some of his most dramatic effects in *Citizen Kane* through cutting. "For my style, for my vision of the cinema," he said, "montage is not an aspect, it is *the* aspect . . . the images themselves are not sufficient; they are very important but they are only images. The essential thing is the duration of each image, and what follows each image. . . . I search for an exact rhythm between one frame and the next." He shows the deterioration of Kane's first marriage through several breakfast scenes, one after the other, almost without dialogue. In the last, the table between the couple has stretched and Kane's wife is reading the rival newspaper.

Welles also used "lightning mixes," in which the sound from one scene continues into the next. Susan playing the piano and singing for Kane in her apartment becomes her singing before him as his wife, beautifully dressed at a grand piano in their home.

Welles said he planned every shot, "then threw all the plans out. The images have to be discovered in the course of work or else they are cold and lack life."

With all his innovation, *Citizen Kane* turned out to be too unusual to be widely popular. RKO drew back and showed less respect for his next film. *The Magnificent Ambersons* is based on a novel by Booth Tarkington, which Welles had already used on his radio show. Welles does not play a role himself, except as the narrator, but the arrogant young George Amberson Minafer (Tim Holt) resembles him, even in the wolfish way he eats.

The film is set at the beginning of the twentieth century. Welles establishes a nostalgic mood with long takes of several minutes, then dissolves, fades, and frames the film in soft focus like an old photograph. It is the story of the leading family of a small midwestern town, who are being displaced by industrialization. George, the young scion, tries to ignore the change and then to fight it off in the person of Eugene Morgan, who has invented an automobile and is courting his widowed mother, Isabel.

From his radio work Welles had learned to use the different volumes of sounds to give depth to the scene. A ten-minute scene, during which Eugene brings his daughter Lucy to the Minafers' ball, is an example of his skill with deep focus and diminishing sound. At the beginning of the scene, the camera moves forward with them as doors open and people step aside. At the end, Eugene and Isabel dance alone in the foreground and George sits talking with Lucy, far off but clearly present.

Welles's own favorite scene takes place in the kitchen. George and his Uncle Jack tease his spinster Aunt Fanny (Agnes Moorehead) about her interest in Eugene until she runs out of the room in tears. Since the camera is still for a change, giving no clues, the viewer has to watch all the characters at once to understand what is being revealed—Fanny's passion and frustration and George's obliviousness as he gobbles her food.

The actors rehearsed this four-and-a-half-minute scene for five weeks, and it took four days to film. According to Welles, "We discussed everybody's life, each one's character, their background, their position at this moment in the story, what they would think about everything—and then sat down and cranked the camera." The actors added some of their own improvised remarks to the script.

Of working with actors, Welles said that "physically, and in the way they develop, I demand the precision of ballet. But their way of acting comes directly from their own ideas as much as from mine." Many actors credit Welles with eliciting their best performances.

Moorehead said of him, "Orson can get an actor to do things he doesn't even know he has it within him to do."

As soon as shooting for *The Magnificent Ambersons* was over, Welles was sent to Brazil to make *It's All True*, a film about Latin America, to be financed partly by the government and partly by RKO. Welles made three segments—one on bullfighting, a history of the samba, and the story of four Brazilian fishermen who became national heroes. Meanwhile he was trying to edit *The Magnificent Ambersons* by phone and mail. But studio executives took it out of his hands. They cut sixty minutes, reshuffled the last two reels, and filmed a new, optimistic ending that was inconsistent with the rest of the film. Welles said of the editing, "It looks as though somebody had run a lawnmower through the celluloid!"

*The Magnificent Ambersons* was finally released as the second half of a double bill, and *It's All True* was never released because no one at the studio understood it. *Journey into Fear* (1943), a spy thriller Welles helped to write, acted in, and supervised at night while he was making *Ambersons*, also failed. Welles's contract with RKO was over, and his star in Hollywood had fallen.

His personal life was in a shambles, too. At nineteen he had married a Chicago socialite and later had a daughter. That marriage, blighted by his unfaithfulness, ended in 1939 just before he left for Hollywood. Then he had a romance with the Mexican film star Dolores Del Rio, who played in *Journey into Fear,* followed by a series of affairs with other actresses. Although Welles married three times, he never had a lasting relationship with a woman. Critics note that many of his female characters are predatory, and Welles himself said, "I hate women, but I need them."

Although he was unwelcome in Hollywood as a director, Welles continued to be popular as a radio and film star and a personality. Rejected by the army because of flat feet and asthma, he contributed to the war effort by making political broadcasts on the radio, writing a newspaper column, and lecturing all over the country about the horrors of fascism. Later, he willingly acted in anything anywhere for money to support his own films. Often he left a location in the middle of shooting in order to replenish his till.

Over the years, Welles acted in sixty-one films, many of them awful. Two roles stand out, however. He played Mr. Rochester in the film version of *Jane Eyre* (1944), as he had done earlier on the radio. Some critics attribute the unusual lighting and direction to his influence. In a mere ten minutes on the screen in the thriller *The Third Man* (1949), he creates a memorable image of the evil Harry Lime. Critics have identified his influence on the style of this film also, and he said that he wrote the speech in which Lime justifies his immoral acts. But movie acting was "sheer agony," according to Welles. "I must call upon an entire complicated mental process to do what Gary Cooper did as easily as breathing."

Welles's next opportunity to direct arose from an acting job. *The Stranger* (1946) is about a Nazi official (Welles) hiding as a prep school teacher in a small American town. Welles liked the script so much that he asked to direct it. The producer agreed but insisted on approval of the final shooting script. Although this was the most profitable of Welles's films, he considered it his worst. "There is nothing of me in that picture," he said. "I did it to prove that I could put out a movie as well as anyone else." The ending, however, in which the Nazi, trapped in a high clock tower, is speared by the sword of a huge revolving figure on the clock, does seem particularly Wellesian.

*The Lady from Shanghai* (1948) was a title Welles

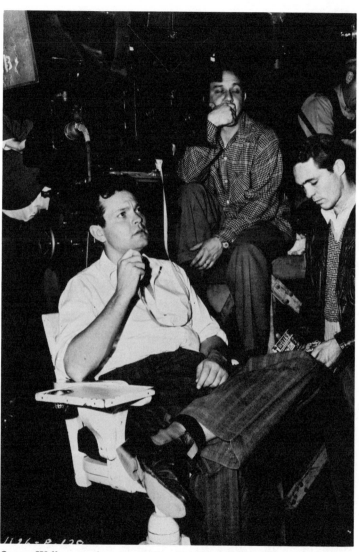

Orson Welles on the set of *The Stranger*, RKO, 1946. *Museum of Modern Art, Film Stills Archive.*

picked from a rack of paperbacks as he was talking to Harry Cohn of Columbia on the phone, trying to get the money to film a musical version of *Around the World in Eighty Days*. He suggested filming it, starring Rita Hayworth, Hollywood's top star and Welles's wife at the time. Cohn agreed and advanced him the money he needed.

When Welles finally read the book, he hated it and rewrote it completely for the film. His confusing screenplay for *The Lady from Shanghai* is about a naïve Irish sailor (Welles) who gets caught up in the plans of a beautiful but evil woman (Hayworth) and her crippled millionaire husband. He agrees to take the blame for a murder that isn't actually supposed to happen, but does.

The studio held up the release of the film, fearing that Hayworth's cold-blooded role would damage her glamorous image. They also cut and changed much of the film, adding close-ups Welles had not shot. But the climax—a shootout in a hall of mirrors—has the richness of many things happening at once that is typical of Welles, and its bizarre quality suits the plot and characters.

Welles next persuaded Republic Films to give him a small budget ($700,000) and twenty-three days to film *Macbeth* (1948). To save time and money, he rehearsed the actors by staging the play at a festival and recorded the sound track in advance. He used a single papier-mâché set, which was shifted for each scene. The film has been criticized for the quality of the acting, including Welles's as Macbeth, for the bad sound track and synchronization, for the use of Scottish accents, and for altering Shakespeare.

Welles defended the film as an experiment, which he hoped would "encourage other filmmakers to tackle difficult subjects at greater speeds." The Scottish burr, he said, was meant to slow the speech of the actors so that audiences unfamiliar with Shakespeare could hear the words. As for the interpretation: "Assuming that the film is an art form, I take the line that you can adapt a classic freely and vigorously for the cinema."

In debt and in trouble with the Internal Revenue Service, Welles went to live in Europe. He did not return to make another film in the United States until 1958.

It took Welles four years to make *Othello* (1952), his first film in Europe. He would stop filming when money ran out and start again when and where he could earn it as an actor. He had to recast several times and then had trouble assembling everyone for filming and making the sound track. He disguised stand-ins in hoods or put their backs to the camera and cross-cut from one character to another when he couldn't get his cast together. He also spoke half the lines himself.

Yet *Othello* shared the Grand Prix at the Cannes Film Festival. It is the visual beauty of the film that has earned it most praise. Critics point, for example, to the scene in which Iago turns Othello against his wife Desdemona. As he listens to Iago's lies, Othello is looking into a circular mirror that distorts his reflection. The staging of another famous scene was an accident: Welles set the attempt on Cassio's life and the murder of Roderigo in a steamy Turkish bath because their costumes had not arrived on time.

Again Welles was called on to justify his loose adaptation. Although it obviously would not exist without Shakespeare, he said, "*Othello* the movie, I hope, is first and foremost a motion picture."

*Mr. Arkadin,* or *Confidential Report* (1955), was adapted from Welles's own novel. Welles plays Gregory Arkadin, an international tycoon, whose power and bulk are emphasized by low camera angles. Arkadin hires a young man supposedly to uncover his past, of which he pretends to have no memory. In fact, he wants him to track down his former associates in a white slave trade so that he can kill them and hide the truth from his daughter (played by Paola Mori, Welles's third wife). When his plan goes awry and he thinks his daughter has found out the truth, Arkadin jumps to his death from his plane. (The film begins with an empty airplane flying above the ocean.)

Welles blamed the producers for the critical drubbing the film suffered. Their cutting and rearranging, he said, made his technical style stand out awkwardly.

Welles returned to America to play Hank Quinlan, a corrupt police captain, in the thriller *Touch of Evil* (1958). But Charlton Heston, who was also starring in the film, insisted that Welles direct as well, and the producer agreed. Welles's first act was to dismiss the screenplay as "ridiculous" and write his own. As an actor—with his paunch, a limp, sweat, and cigars—Welles created a rich character, both repulsive and compelling. As a director, he used extreme-angle shots and other techniques to create a disturbing atmosphere.

Welles's next film was *The Trial* (1962), based on the novel by Franz Kafka about a man trapped in an absurd legal bureaucracy. This was the first Welles film since *Citizen Kane* that was released exactly as he intended it. It was not free of problems, however. Halfway through, the producers told him that they could not afford the promised studio. Welles found a replacement—the deserted railroad station he had been looking at from his hotel window. To save money, he not only wrote, directed, and acted in the film but was the second cameraman and the editor and dubbed the voices of eleven characters.

Continental European critics hailed the film, but the Americans and the British generally disliked it, some finding it unbearably grim. Welles was also criticized for altering the intent of the original by changing the ending. Welles's Joseph K throws back the sticks of dynamite that are tossed down on him in his trench. "I couldn't put my name to a work that implies man's ultimate surrender," Welles said.

Welles called his next film, *Falstaff* or *Chimes at Midnight* (1966), "the story of the betrayal of friendship." The friendship is between Henry IV's son Prince Hal and his lusty companion Falstaff, whom he abandons when he becomes king. The story is drawn from the various Shakespearean plays in which the character of Falstaff appears. Welles said of him, "He is the character in whom I believe the most. The most entirely good man in all drama."

Most critics consider *Falstaff* Welles's most successful production of Shakespeare and his best performance as an actor. When it was screened at the Cannes Film Festival, Welles won a special award for his contribution to world cinema. It is a beautiful film with excellent acting, although the sound track is badly synchronized. The cutting, camera movement, and composition subtly convey Welles's meaning without calling attention to themselves. He used a still camera, for instance, for Henry's speeches and a moving one for Falstaff's.

The Battle of Shrewsbury sequence has been praised for its rhythmic montage. Although it seems to be composed of hundreds of quick shots, Welles actually cut them from long takes he had made to ensure that the actors would always be warmed up. It took him two and a half weeks to assemble this sequence.

After *Falstaff*, Welles directed various projects that he either left unfinished or never released. He did finish two short films, however. *The Immortal Story* (1967) is based on a short story by the Danish writer Isak Dinesen. *F is for Fake* (1973) is a semidocumentary about art and forgery, among other things, with a flashy editing style.

But Welles pinned his hopes for a comeback on a major film he had been shooting off and on since the summer of 1970: *The Other Side of the Wind.* This was to be a satire of Hollywood, which Welles wrote himself, and shot in a style which used everything from still pictures to 35-millimeter color film. In it John Huston plays an old-time director who tries to make a modish film but ends up killing himself in a car crash.

Orson Welles won the Life Achievement Award from the American Film Institute, the D. W. Griffith Award from the Directors Guild, and an honorary Oscar. He accepted such honors, he said, "not for what I have done—but for what I hope to do." Welles died suddenly of a heart attack on October 10, 1985, before he could finish his film and realize that hope.

# JOHN HUSTON

 don't think of myself as simply, uniquely and forever a director of motion pictures," John Huston wrote in his autobiography in 1981. "It is something for which I have a certain talent and a profession the disciplines of which I have mastered over the years, but I also have a certain talent for other things, and I have worked at those disciplines as well." Huston's other talents include painting, writing, acting, boxing, riding, and gambling.

John Huston is the son of the popular theater and film actor Walter Huston. When John was born on August 5, 1906, his father had just left an unsuccessful vaudeville career to be chief engineer at a water and power plant in Nevada, Missouri. Huston claims they went to Nevada when his grandfather won it in a poker game and that they left—quickly—after his father turned the water valve the wrong way during a terrible fire and half the town burned down.

In any case, when John was three his father left his mother and returned to the stage. John went with his mother to Los Angeles, where she resumed her former career as a newspaperwoman. His childhood was spent on the road, shuttling between his parents and touring with his father. Over the years, relations with his mother became strained, but "my father and I were as close as a father and son can be. He was my companion and friend."

When John was about twelve, he was discovered to have an enlarged heart and some symptoms of kidney disease. Although his heart was no larger than it should be for a boy who would grow to be a very large man, and the symptoms were mild, he was diagnosed as having a terminal illness, and sent to a sanitarium. He was released after several months, however, when the doctors learned that every night he was sneaking out to swim in an icy stream nearby above a steep, stony waterfall.

This yearning for action and risk stayed with John Huston. At the age of fifteen he dropped out of school to become a professional boxer. He claims to have won twenty-three out of twenty-five fights, but quit after his nose was permanently flattened. He later returned to this scene of small-time boxing in central California with *Fat City* (1972), a depressing, unpopular film that the critics praised. Except for the leads—Jeff Bridges and Stacy Keach—most of the actors were old boxing acquaintances of Huston's or people he had found on location. "I had a great interest in the characters," Huston said. "Personally I admire the down-and-outers depicted in the film. People who have the heroism to go on taking it on the chin in life as well as in the ring."

When he was eighteen, John went to New York to watch his father rehearse for Eugene O'Neill's *Desire under the Elms*. O'Neill joined Kipling, Joyce, and Hemingway in Huston's literary pantheon. "I think I learned more about films from O'Neill than anyone—what a scene consists of, and so forth." He decided then that he wanted to be an actor, and his father helped him get his first role.

About this time, he married a girl he knew from high school. The marriage lasted less than a year. She was the first of five wives, several of whom complained that even when married, Huston continued to act like a bachelor. His longest-lasting marriage was to Ricki Soma, a ballet dancer hired by MGM. He was forty-three when they married; she was nineteen, and seven months pregnant. Marilyn Monroe, who had her first speaking part in a Huston film (*Asphalt Jungle*, 1950) and starred in *The Misfits* (1961), attested to his attractiveness: "I just don't see how any woman could be around John Huston without falling in love with him."

Even before his first marriage had ended, Huston, who loved to ride, decided to join the Mexican Army so that he could do it for free. In two years he was a lieutenant, and enjoying champagne, poker, brothels, and outrageous exploits. He was also developing an enduring love for Mexico that would keep drawing him back.

While there, he wrote a play and some stories about gambling, horses, and boxing, modeling them on Hemingway's lean style. He sold the play and a short story but quickly spent the money. This has been the pattern of his finances throughout his career—fortunes won and lost, money from tomorrow paying today's rent. He blames his mother, who bet on the horses. "She taught me that money's for spending, and to hell with the odds."

When he returned from Mexico, his father got him a job as a dialogue writer, and his mother got him a job on her paper, though he admits to being "the world's lousiest reporter." In the story that got him fired, he reversed the names of a murderer and his victim.

In 1929 Huston was hired as a contract writer by Goldwyn Studios, but he was given no work. After six months, he left for a job at Universal, his father's studio. He wrote three or four films, then went to London to work for Gaumont-British, where again there was no work. Again he quit. After he used up all his money (including a hundred pounds he had won in the Irish Sweepstakes), he sang cowboy songs on the street for a living and slept in Hyde Park.

He then went to Paris for a year to study painting. To support himself, he drew pictures of tourists at sidewalk cafés. He had attended art school briefly after high school and later would say that "nothing has played a more important role in my life." It taught him, he says, how to use lighting to capture a mood and also how to arrange people and objects within a frame. He often gives four films as examples.

*The Red Badge of Courage* (1951), according to Huston, was the first film to which he was able to apply his interest in photography and art. He took his style from the Civil War photographs of Matthew Brady. "I tried to reproduce the feel of the photographs with a kind of bleached effect, because originally they were made by wet plate photography."

In several other films, Huston experimented with color. "Artistically," he said, "I am most concerned with controlling the color. . . . Color, like camera acrobatics, can be a distraction unless it's functional in the film." Huston agreed with the critics of his *Moulin Rouge* (1952), about Toulouse-Lautrec, that the color photography was the most successful aspect of the romanticized story of the painter's life. "I was going to use color on the screen as Lautrec had used it in his paintings. Our idea was to flatten the color, render it in planes of solid hues, do away with the highlights and the illusion of third dimension."

For *Moby Dick* (1956) he worked out a way of adding black and white to color. He wanted the film to look like nineteenth-century steel engravings of sailing ships and also to have an ominous tone.

Huston wanted "poetic" color for the psychological film *Reflections in a Golden Eye* (1967) by the southern writer Carson McCullers. He used sepialike hues until the murder at the end, which is shown in full Technicolor. But after the first poor reviews, the studio replaced his print with an ordinary Technicolor one.

Huston's career as a screenwriter finally took off. At the age of thirty-five he was a contract writer at Warner's with a growing reputation. He had written two highly regarded screenplays: *Sergeant York* for Howard Hawks and *High Sierra* for Raoul Walsh.

But Huston wanted to direct, and he put a clause in his contract ensuring that he would get that opportunity. "It wasn't to protect my writing," he said, "in the way I am told other writers have proceeded; it was simply the desire to direct. Directing is just an extension of the writing. They're not different departments." What the director does is "put in the things that are between the lines of dialogue." Although he was rarely on the set as a writer, he said, "directing was something that came instinctively. I knew almost exactly what I was going to do."

For most of his films, Huston either wrote the screenplay himself, based on a novel or story, or shared the job with another writer. "The writer will do a scene and then I'll work it over or I'll write a scene and then the other writer will make adjustments later. Often we trade scenes back and forth until we're both satisfied." Some collaborators were professional screenwriters. Others included critic James Agee *(The African Queen)*, novelist

Truman Capote *(Beat the Devil)*, science fiction writer Ray Bradbury *(Moby Dick)*, playwright Arthur Miller *(The Misfits)*, and philosopher Jean-Paul Sartre *(Freud)*.

Huston chose *The Maltese Falcon* by Dashiell Hammett as his directorial debut in 1941, although Warner's already had produced two unsuccessful versions. Huston co-authored the script about Sam Spade, a hard-boiled detective (played by Humphrey Bogart) who is drawn into the scheme of a group of characters trying to get hold of a valuable statuette. The studio expected a routine gangster picture and gave him a short shooting schedule and a small budget. What they got instead is a film many critics consider the best crime picture ever made, with classic examples of camera style and pacing. It also was a tremendous hit.

For the screenplay Huston deliberately stayed close to the book. "I attempted to transpose Hammett's highly individual prose style into camera terms with sharp photography, geographically exact camera movements, and striking, if not shocking, set ups." He also tried to present the film, like the book, from Spade's point of view. Spade appears in every scene except the one in which his partner is murdered, and the other characters are introduced as they meet him.

This faithfulness to the original has continued to be the basis of Huston's technical and artistic style, or nonstyle, as he sees it: "If there is a style, it's to adapt myself to the material consistently, and as it changes in each film, so does the style. I see each picture I make as being totally different from any other."

Because it was his first time directing, Huston prepared for *The Maltese Falcon* very carefully. He made hundreds of drawings of set construction, camera angles, and the positions of actors. He never did that again, and by 1982 advised an interviewer, "Rehearse and observe the scene, be patient with yourself, and discover the

Humphrey Bogart, Peter Lorre, Mary Astor, and Sydney Greenstreet in *The Maltese Falcon*, Warner Brothers, 1941. *Museum of Modern Art, Film Stills Archive.*

introductory shot. When you've found the first shot, the rest follows suit. There's what amounts to a grammar." Now he makes drawings only when the art department needs them, as for action scenes with the mechanical whales in *Moby Dick*.

In spite of the careful preparations for his first film, Huston encouraged the actors to work out scenes for themselves. Finding that they usually either fell into his plans or invented something better, he adopted this approach throughout his career. He now rarely instructs actors about gestures or delivery. But in *The Maltese Falcon*, because he wanted Brigid O'Shaughnessy to sound nervous when she was lying to Spade, he had the actress Mary Astor run around the set a few times so that she would be slightly breathless.

The film created a new image for Humphrey Bogart, who starred in five more Huston films: *Across the Pacific* (1942), *The Treasure of the Sierra Madre* (1948), *Key Largo* (1948), *The African Queen* (1951), and *Beat the Devil* (1954). Huston brought out his humor and the combination of tenderness and toughness for which he is famous. Bogart says to Mary Astor when he turns her over to the police, "Yes, Angel, I'm going to send you over. The chances are you'll get off with life. . . . I'll be waiting for you. If they hang you, I'll always remember you."

Huston's next two films before going into the army were notable mainly for noncinematic reasons. A romance with Olivia de Havilland, one of the stars of the melodrama *In This Our Life* (1942), broke up his second marriage. And he played one of his most famous pranks on the director who replaced him on *Across the Pacific* (1942) when he had to report for duty. This is a war picture in which Bogart outwits a spy for the Japanese. Before Huston left, "I had Bogie tied to a chair, and installed almost three times as many Japanese soldiers as were needed to keep him prisoner. . . . I made it so that there was no way in God's green world that Bogart could logically escape."

Huston called his time in the army "the most compelling experience of my life." He saw the war first-hand, gathering footage for his documentaries, and learned to admire the American soldier for "facing death with dignity."

From this experience he developed a preference, uncommon at that time, for shooting on location. "I found a freedom and an inspiration from a location that the barren walls of a Hollywood studio don't give me. . . . The kind of stories which have appealed to me over the years since the war take place out of doors in remote regions." His locations have always been an important aspect of his films, closely tied to their themes.

Huston's last film for the army, *Let There Be Light*, inspired his later film biography of Sigmund Freud. It documented the rehabilitation of soldiers at a mental hospital on Long Island and was meant to encourage companies to hire these men. But the government decided not to publicize the psychological casualties of the war, and the film wasn't released until 1980. At that time it was called a masterpiece, and Huston recalled that making it was "like having a religious experience."

Some critics consider his next feature film, *The Treasure of the Sierra Madre* (1948), his best. It won Academy Awards for Best Director and Best Screenplay, and Walter Huston won as Best Supporting Actor. Huston had chosen the novel on which this film is based partly because he thought the role of Howard, the experienced old prospector, was ideal for his father.

Like many Huston films to follow, *Sierra Madre* is about a small group of people on a quest, and focuses less on the quest itself than on the interactions of the characters. Three men (Bogart, Walter Huston, and Tim Holt) go into the Sierra Madre searching for gold. They find it, but their greed works on their characters. In a tragic, ironic ending, the gold that had destroyed them blows away. Huston said in his autobiography about this selection of material: "Certain themes trigger a deeper personal response than others, and success stories, per se, are not really of much interest to me."

The authentic Mexican location Huston chose for *Sierra Madre* was a land of hills and blazing sun overrun with insects and reptiles. He went even further for *The African Queen* (1951), his most popular and financially successful film and the one for which Humphrey Bogart won an Oscar. It was filmed in what is now Zaire, about 1,100 miles up the Congo River. The various dangers and

John Huston on location for *The Treasure of the Sierra Madre,*
Warner Brothers, 1948. *Museum of Modern Art, Film Stills Archive.*

discomforts included an attack by an army of carnivorous ants, which forced the film company to move. But Huston insisted, "I had to do this film on location. I wanted these characters to sweat when the script called for it."

Pauline Kael hailed *The African Queen* as "one of the most charming and entertaining movies ever made." Its humor, as in most of Huston's films, comes from the characters rather than from the story line. Rose Sayer (Katharine Hepburn), a spinster missionary, and Charlie Allnut (Bogart), an unshaven, gin-swizzling boat captain, are thrown together on his mail boat, *The African Queen*, when the Germans land in Africa. Their original attempt to escape turns into a plot to attack an enemy warship by turning the *Queen* into a torpedo. Charlie and Rosie fall in love after defying death together as they pass through the river's virtually unnavigable rapids, but they are captured. Their marriage ceremony is performed by the German captain: "I pronounce you man and wife. Proceed with the execution."

Huston credited the combination of Bogart and Hepburn for the success of the film. "One brought out a vein of humor in the other," he said. Yet it was he who gave Hepburn the key to her character when she was acting too coldly toward Bogart. He advised her to use Eleanor Roosevelt as her model.

Because he is often the writer as well as the director of his films, Huston knows his characters well and can share his understanding with the actors when they need help. In *Key Largo* (1948), for instance, Claire Trevor plays a third-rate nightclub singer. She has been resurrected by her former gangster boyfriend who is trying to make his own comeback. Huston told her: "You're the kind of drunken dame whose elbows are a little too big. Your voice is a little too loud, you're a little too polite. You're very sad, very resigned."

Huston also uses his acting skills in directing.

Deborah Kerr (*The Night of the Iguana*, 1964) said of him, "He's a superb actor . . . and can show you so vividly what he wants you to achieve." In that film, Ava Gardner, having fought with the man she really loves, goes swimming with some beachboys. Before she played the scene, Huston acted it out in the water himself.

Generally, however, Huston defers to the actors in everything but dialogue. He concentrates on finding the right actors. "I believe the most important part of picture making is the casting—matching the actor to the proper character and making sure the actor understands the character."

With *The African Queen*, which was filmed in Europe and Africa with British technicians and many British actors, Huston became an international filmmaker, though one who made clearly American films. In late 1952, he moved away from the United States, taking his family to live in Ireland, the home of his paternal grandparents. He said that his distaste for the Communist witch-hunts of the McCarthy era influenced his decision to leave the country, but so did Ireland's favorable tax laws for artists. In 1964 he became an Irish citizen. Huston comfortably adopted the life of a country squire and hunted foxes as Joint Master of the Galway Blazers for ten years.

He stayed there until 1972, when he married his fifth wife. Because she hated Ireland, they moved to Mexico. When they left, Houston said, "I sometimes feel that I sold a little bit of my soul." The marriage ended after three years, but Huston stayed in Mexico. He now lives in a compound of six elaborate huts he designed himself, fifteen miles south of Puerto Vallarta and accessible only by jungle trails. "I wake before dawn," he said, "and see the miracle occur. Then there's fishing, or swimming or my writing. It's just exactly what I wanted. A place that will see me out."

Huston always read voraciously, even as a child, and some of his films are based on works of literature that are dear to him. As a result, they stay respectfully close to the original. The first of these was Stephen Crane's *The Red Badge of Courage*, the story of a young boy's first experience in battle. Huston said it was "about the psychology of courage. It demonstrates how cowardice and courage are really composed of the same material." It is also a kind of quest, less important for its product than its process. Passing soldiers tell the youth at the end that he wasn't even in the day's major battle.

The actors Huston used for this film were mainly nonprofessionals. Audie Murphy, World War II's most decorated soldier, played the youth, and Huston sent to poolrooms for tough-looking extras. "They had the quality of the characters, which is more important to me," he said. Because he works so much on location, Huston has to be able to respond to the unexpected. "I try to let the whole thing work on me. The actors, the set, the locations, the sounds . . . ," he has said. "Everything that happens in the process of making the film can contribute to the development of that film's story."

This flexibility is part of his style. Shooting *The Red Badge of Courage*, he noticed that the actor chosen to slip and get shot was wearing glasses. Huston used him for a dramatic close-up: after being hit, he fumbles for his glasses, adjusts them around his ears, and dies.

The film fared poorly in previews, partly because its anti-war sentiment was unsuited to the period of the Korean War. The producers cut, re-edited, and added a narration to the film after Huston had finished. This rarely happens to Huston's films, since he edits with the camera, requiring few takes, so that "as a rule, there's only one way to put my stuff together."

Huston dreamed of making a movie of *Moby Dick* for more than a decade. The 1956 film, he said, was the "most difficult picture I ever made." First, he had to condense a complex work of art into a two-hour film. Then he had to contend with mechanical whales that either escaped or broke down in the rough seas around Wales, where he was filming.

As always, Huston was a stickler for details, insisting on authenticity. Captian Ahab, for example, has to have a whalebone peg leg that looked as if it had been made at sea. The tiller of his ship, the *Pequod*, had to be made of the skull of a killer whale and the jawbone of a sperm whale, as in the novel. He also took his cast to Madeira to go on a real whale hunt.

The film took two years to shoot and cost $4.5 million, but was not a big moneymaker. Critics praised the color and technical effects but thought Gregory Peck was too dispassionate to play Captain Ahab. Huston disagreed and staunchly defended his choice: "I myself felt that Peck brought a superb dignity to the role. . . . What many people had seen in the original Barrymore version of *Moby Dick* had led them to expect an Ahab of wild gestures and staring eyes: that wasn't Melville."

Huston first read Rudyard Kipling's novels, stories, and poems when he was confined to bed as a young boy. "I read so much Kipling, it's in my unconscious," he once said. One story—"The Man Who Would Be King"—especially haunted him. For more than twenty years he thought about making it into a movie, first with his father, then with Humphrey Bogart and Clark Gable, then with Peter O'Toole and Richard Burton. Finally, in 1975, it came to be, starring Michael Caine and Sean Connery.

Collaborating with his long-time assistant, Gladys Hill, Huston kept the screenplay as true as possible to Kipling. But since the story is only twenty-five pages long, they had to add dialogue. Also, because it is written in the first person, they added Kipling as a character.

The critic Brendan Gill found the screenplay "far superior" to the original.

The story is about two former British soldiers who set out from India for an uncharted country where they can rule as gods. They succeed until one of them is exposed as a mortal. He is killed, the gold they accumulated as tribute is lost (much as in *Treasure of the Sierra Madre*), and the survivor returns to Kipling in rags, carrying his partner's shrunken head.

This was Huston's first epic, shot in Morocco with more than 150 actors, 100 vehicles, and about 500 local extras. Critics praised it unanimously, John Simon calling it "John Huston's best film in twenty-three years, or since *African Queen*."

In 1977 Huston suffered an aneurism of the aorta and had to have open heart surgery. But before long he was back at work. In 1980 he directed a film of Flannery O'Connor's strange story "Wise Blood," about a young religious fanatic. It premiered at the Cannes Film Festival as part of a tribute to Huston and received good reviews. He then made two films in Canada and the film version of the musical *Annie* (1982), which was panned; critics saw it as a movie event rather than a movie, and noted that it had little of Huston in it.

He rebounded, however, with two critical successes. *Under the Volcano* (1984) is an adaptation of a complex novel by Malcolm Lowry. It shows a single day in the life of the British consul to Mexico in 1938. "The Consul," Huston said, "is the most complicated character I've ever had in a film."

Although he did not write the script himself, Huston spent ten hours of every day for two months working on it. According to the screenwriter, "John pushed toward a very clear intention in every scene." The film was shot mostly in sequence, which Huston prefers because it gives the filming the rhythm of storytelling. He worked regularly until three or four in the morning and on the last night of shooting from sunset to dawn. Critics expressed their respect for his ability to shape this very difficult material into a film. Huston himself said that Albert Finney's performance as the consul was "the finest performance I've ever witnessed, let along directed."

*Prizzi's Honor* (1985) is a black comedy about a hit man for the Mafia (Jack Nicholson) who falls for a fellow professional (Kathleen Turner). The director's daughter, Anjelica Huston, plays Maerose Prizzi, Nicholson's former girl friend, in a heavy Brooklyn accent ("the voice of the movie," Huston told his actors). When the film premiered at the Venice Film Festival, Huston was awarded a Golden Lion for "the entirety of his work," and Anjelica Huston won an Oscar for Best Supporting Actress.

Besides writing twenty-seven films and directing thirty-nine, in some of which he makes a brief appearance, Huston also appeared as a character actor in more than two dozen films, most of them less distinguished than his own—for example, *The Battle for the Planet of the Apes*, in which he played the Gorilla Sage. His most prominent role was as Faye Dunaway's evil millionaire father in *Chinatown*, and he was nominated for an Academy Award as Best Supporting Actor in Otto Preminger's *The Cardinal*. But Huston has always said that he does not take acting seriously, that he does it for the money and because it is much easier than directing. "Being in front of the camera without any responsibility whatever is a welcome change."

At the age of eighty, John Huston talks eagerly about projects in the offing. "My hero is Renoir," he said. "He sat in a chair and painted until his last day. I think he was eighty-three. I want to keep right on going until my momentum winds down and I fall out of this chair."

# AFTERWORD

By what standard, readers are entitled to ask, were the ten directors in this book chosen as "great"? There is more than one answer.

One measure of greatness is the amount of pleasure their movies still bring when they are shown forty, fifty, sixty, or more years after they were made. We are charmed by the sparks that fly between Katharine Hepburn and Spencer Tracy in George Cukor's *Adam's Rib* and *Pat and Mike*. We are moved by the visions of America in Frank Capra's *It's a Wonderful Life* and John Ford's *Wagonmaster*. We laugh and cry with Chaplin's Tramp in *The Kid* and *The Gold Rush*. And we gasp with delight at the blind chase of Keaton and his girl around the boat in *The Navigator*.

When Alfred Hitchcock's *Rear Window* and *Vertigo* were re-released in 1985 for the first time in many years, crowds lined up in front of theaters that usually show first-run movies. And it is an annual tradition at Harvard University to forget exam-time miseries by attending a popular Humphrey Bogart festival featuring John Huston's *The African Queen* and Howard Hawks's *To Have and Have Not.*

Another measure of greatness is the influence these directors of the past had on one another and on later film directors. Here, the name D. W. Griffith is preeminent, in Europe as well as in America. "Nothing essential has been added to the art of the film since Griffith," said the French director René Clair. Frank Capra used virtually the same words in his eulogy for Griffith: "Since Griffith there has been no major improvement in the art of film direction." And there is no director alive who would deny Griffith's influence on filmmaking all over the world.

Among the other directors in this book, only Orson Welles evokes such sweeping praise from his fellows. Nicholas Ray, an American director of the 1950s, wrote that Welles "is one of the greatest directors in the history of cinema, and all of us who are trying to direct movies owe him a debt for the many new paths he pioneered." And Jean-Luc Godard, the French director, wrote, "May we be accursed if we forget for one second that he alone with Griffith, one in silent days, one sound, managed to start up that marvelous little electric train. . . . All of us always will owe him everything."

But Welles had his own tribute to make. "John Ford was my teacher," he said. "My own style has nothing to do with his, but *Stagecoach* was my movie textbook. I ran it over forty times." Howard Hawks was another admirer of Ford. When asked whether he was influenced by Ford, he said that he didn't know how anyone could make a Western without being influenced by John Ford. He was also pleased that in *Red River,* his first Western, he was able to capture a Ford-like effect: a cloud passes in front of the sun while John Wayne stands praying over a grave. Ford, in his turn, credited Hawks's *Red River* with convincing him that John Wayne could really act.

Charlie Chaplin and Alfred Hitchcock established their own filmmaking domains. Chaplin gave film comedy a legitimacy it didn't have before. His combination of humor and pathos also set a standard that filmmakers like Woody Allen are still measured against today. "With Keaton he was the master of us all," said Jacques Tati, the great French comedian, after Chaplin's death.

Hitchcock legitimized the suspense genre as an art. The French filmmaker and critic François Truffaut said of him that if a director "sets out to make a thriller or a suspense picture, you may be certain that in his heart of hearts he is hoping to live up to one of Hitchcock's masterpieces."

It is hard to imagine today, with our film courses, and revival movie theaters, and the availability of old movies on television and videocassette, that movies were originally made for immediate consumption, not to be shown ever again once their run was over. Only with the arrival of television as a greedy new market in the 1950s did the studios dust off the forgotten treasures in their closets. And only because of the vocal interest of a group of young French filmmakers and critics in the 1950s did many American directors begin to be recognized as artists. Thus, the filmmakers who were working in the 1970s were the first directors to grow up with a history of American movies in which to immerse themselves.

One of them, Martin Scorsese, remembers loving Westerns as a child. "John Ford is my favorite director," he said. "I love all of his films. . . . I began to develop a critical awareness when I realized that most of these films were made by the same people. There was usually John Wayne in the movie, Maureen O'Hara, and Henry

Fonda." Scorsese used clips from *The Searchers* as a tribute to Ford in *Who's That Knocking?* and *Mean Streets*. George Cukor was another influence. Scorsese's musical *New York, New York* has some of the dark overtones of Cukor's *A Star Is Born*, and in fact the older director was with him on the set during shooting.

Brian De Palma was called the Hitchcock of the seventies, and has been accused of imitating the master. He insists that he has his own style but that Hitchcock "found the kind of scenarios that work best. So, when you work in the suspense form, you're almost forced to use some of the ideas he pioneered. He's like a grammar book." In the first half of *Dressed to Kill*, De Palma uses the Hitchcock technique of telling his story with the camera instead of with dialogue. He also sets his climax in a brightly lit room rather than in the darkness usually associated with crime. His model was the terrifying scene in Hitchcock's *North by Northwest* in which Cary Grant is chased beneath a beautiful clear sky by a crop-dusting plane on a mission to kill him.

Maybe the most important measure of "greatness," however, is in these directors' ability to draw others to their craft. Peter Bogdanovitch said that seeing Orson Welles's *Citizen Kane* was what made him want to be a director. And François Truffaut said that *"Citizen Kane* has inspired more vocations to cinema throughout the world than any other film."

# SELECTED BIBLIOGRAPHY

Some of the general books listed here are histories. Others include chapters about some of the directors in this book.

Listed under the name of each director are the books I found most interesting and useful. Many of them include complete filmographies.

## GENERAL

Everson, William K. **The American Movie.** New York: Atheneum, 1963.

**The Hollywood Professionals** (series). New York: A. S. Barnes, 1973–1980. Volume 3 (1974), edited by John Belton, contains chapter on Hawks; volume 6 (1980), edited by Allen Estrin, contains chapters on Capra and Cukor.

Mast, Gerald. **A Short History of the Movies.** New York: Pegasus, 1971.

Sarris, Andrew. **The American Cinema: Directors and Directions 1929–1968.** New York: Dutton, 1968. Includes short biographies of all directors in this book.

Sarris, Andrew. **Hollywood Voices: Interviews with Film Directors.** Indianapolis: Bobbs-Merrill, 1971. Interviews with Cukor, Huston, and Welles.

Schickel, Richard. **The Men Who Made the Movies.** New York: Atheneum, 1975. Interviews with Capra, Cukor, Hawks, and Hitchcock.

## FRANK CAPRA

Capra, Frank. **The Name above the Title: An Autobiography.** New York: Macmillan, 1971.

Glatzer, Richard, and John Raeburn, eds. **Frank Capra: The Man and His Films.** Ann Arbor: University of Michigan Press, 1975.

Maland, Charles J. **Frank Capra.** Boston: Twayne, 1980.

Poague, Leland A. **The Cinema of Frank Capra: An Approach to Film Comedy.** New York: A. S. Barnes, 1975.

## CHARLES CHAPLIN

Chaplin, Charles. **My Autobiography.** New York: Simon & Schuster, 1964.

Huff, Theodore. **Charlie Chaplin.** New York: Henry Schuman, 1951.

Manvell, Roger. **Chaplin.** Boston: Little, Brown, 1974.

McCabe, John. **Charlie Chaplin.** Garden City, N.Y.: Doubleday, 1978.

McCaffrey, Donald W., ed. **Focus on Chaplin.** Englewood
    Cliffs, N.J.: Prentice-Hall, 1971.

Robinson, David. **Chaplin: His Life and Art.** New York:
    McGraw-Hill, 1985.

## GEORGE CUKOR

Carey, Gary. **Cukor & Co.: The Films of George Cukor and
    His Collaborators.** New York: Museum of Modern
    Art, 1971.

Clarens, Carlos. **George Cukor.** London: Secker and
    Warburg, 1976.

Lambert, Gavin. **On Cukor.** New York: Putnam, 1972.

Phillips, Gene D. **George Cukor.** Boston: Twayne, 1982.

## JOHN FORD

Anderson, Lindsay. **About John Ford.** New York: McGraw-
    Hill, 1981.

Bogdanovich, Peter. **John Ford.** Berkeley: University of
    California Press, 1978.

McBride, Joseph, and Michael Wilmington. **John Ford.** New
    York: Da Capo, 1975.

Sarris, Andrew. **The John Ford Movie Mystery.**
    Bloomington: Indiana University Press, 1975.

Sinclair, Andrew. **John Ford.** New York: Dial Press, 1979.

## D. W. GRIFFITH

Barry, Iris. **D. W. Griffith: American Film Master.** Garden
    City, N.Y.: Museum of Modern Art, 1940; reprint
    Doubleday, 1965.

Geduld, Harry M., ed. **Focus on D. W. Griffith.** Englewood Cliffs, N.J.: Prentice-Hall, 1971.

Henderson, Robert M. **D. W. Griffith: His Life and Work.** New York: Oxford University Press, 1972.

Schickel, Richard. **D. W. Griffith: An American Life.** New York: Simon & Schuster, 1984.

Williams, Martin. **Griffith: First Artist of the Movies.** New York: Oxford University Press, 1980.

## HOWARD HAWKS

Bogdanovich, Peter. **The Cinema of Howard Hawks.** New York: Museum of Modern Art, 1962.

Mast, Gerald. **Howard Hawks, Storyteller.** New York: Oxford University Press, 1982.

McBride, Joseph, ed. **Focus on Howard Hawks.** Englewood Cliffs, N.J.: Prentice-Hall, 1972.

McBride, Joseph. **Hawks on Hawks.** Berkeley: University of California Press, 1982.

## ALFRED HITCHCOCK

Spoto, Donald. **The Dark Side of Genius.** Boston: Little, Brown, 1983.

Taylor, John Russell. **Hitch: The Life and Times of Alfred Hitchcock.** New York: Pantheon, 1978.

Truffaut, François, with Helen G. Scott. **Hitchcock.** New York: Simon & Schuster, 1967.

Wood, Robin. **Hitchcock's Films.** New York: A. S. Barnes, 1977.

## JOHN HUSTON

Hammen, Scott. **John Huston.** Boston: Twayne, 1985.

Huston, John. **An Open Book.** New York: Knopf, 1980.

Kaminsky, Stuart. **John Huston: Maker of Magic.** Boston: Houghton Mifflin, 1978.

Madsen, Axel. **John Huston.** New York: Doubleday, 1978.

Pratley, Gerald. **The Cinema of John Huston.** New York: A. S. Barnes, 1977.

## BUSTER KEATON

Blesh, Rudi. **Keaton.** New York: Macmillan, 1966.

Dardis, Tom. **Keaton: The Man Who Wouldn't Lie Down.** New York: Scribner's, 1979.

Keaton, Buster, with Charles Samuels. **My Wonderful World of Slapstick.** Garden City, N.Y.: Doubleday, 1960.

Robinson, David. **Buster Keaton.** London: Secker and Warburg, 1969.

## ORSON WELLES

Bazin, André. **Orson Welles: A Critical View.** New York: Harper & Row, 1978.

Cowie, Peter. **A Ribbon of Dreams: The Cinema of Orson Welles.** New York: A. S. Barnes, 1973.

Gottesman, Ronald, ed. **Focus on Orson Welles.** Englewood Cliffs, N.J.: Prentice-Hall, 1976.

Leaming, Barbara. **Orson Welles.** New York: Viking, 1985.

McBride, Joseph. **Orson Welles: Actor and Director.** New York: Harvest/Harcourt Brace Jovanovich, 1977.

Noble, Peter. **The Fabulous Orson Welles.** London: Hutchinson, 1956.

# INDEX

# ABOUT THE AUTHOR

Dian G. Smith is a freelance writer with a master's degree in education from Harvard University. Her articles have appeared in many national publications and she is the author of three other books for young adults: *Careers in the Visual Arts: Talking with Professionals,* *Women in Finance,* and *American Filmmakers Today.* She inherited her interest in the movies from her great-uncle, Daniel Robins, who opened the Bijou Nickelodeon in Youngstown, Ohio, in 1904.